Your Washington

Your Washington

BY TRISTRAM COFFIN
EDITED BY GORDON CARROLL

Duell, Sloan and Pearce · New York
Little, Brown and Company · Boston

The author wishes to thank *Coronet* for permission to use
pieces which first appeared there.

DUELL, SLOAN AND PEARCE — LITTLE, BROWN
BOOKS ARE PUBLISHED BY
LITTLE, BROWN AND COMPANY
IN ASSOCIATION WITH
DUELL, SLOAN & PEARCE, INC.

Published simultaneously
in Canada by Little, Brown and Company *Limited*

PRINTED IN THE UNITED STATES OF AMERICA

Foreword

A citizen of Moose, Wyoming, writes to the editor of a Washington newspaper:

> *. . . Washington is more than just another city, it is* Our Capital. *. . . In a very real sense, Washington can reflect all the noblest aspirations of our people . . . the character of the city itself can inspire us toward a high purpose in formulating public policy . . . an awareness of the importance of government . . . Cherish these treasures and thereby give leadership to the rest of our country.*

It is easy to understand, therefore, why the author of this book sees in the orderly pattern of Washington's superb natural setting, beautiful gardens, classic architecture, heroic sculpture and durable institutions — the living spirit of a great nation.

Behind the heavy doors of the halls of government, he finds men at work upon the tasks that guide our national destinies and shape our personal lives with a patriotic fervor such as that which inspired our founding fathers. In Washington's marble halls, he sees a conqueror pleading for conciliation, justice and charity; a giant defending the weak and insuring the dignity of its individuals through the institution of government by the consent of the governed. In bronze and stone, he finds the symbols of hope, opportunity and unity that are our national strength; and the immortal words that reawaken our ideals and our faith.

In the rebuilding of the city after destruction by a wanton foe, he senses the indomitable spirit of a free people; in its expansion and growth, the power of the nation. The annual pilgrimages of millions of Americans to this shrine of patriotic veneration reveal devotion to the principles of justice and equality upon which our nation was founded — and their ultimate objective, "peace among ourselves and with all nations."

In beauty of design, perfection of structural details, in museums of science and history, repositories of art and literature and in temples of religion, the author finds an expression of our cultural aspirations and spiritual achievements. In the hurly-burly of everyday living — the sensitive human touch.

This is the Washington that Mr. Coffin has placed within the covers of his book. It is the Washington of the citizens of Moose, Wyoming, and the citizens of every other state, city and hamlet. It is the privilege and the duty of every American to know his National Capital, and for those who have not yet had the opportunity of visiting Washington, Mr. Coffin has performed an important service.

EDWARD J. KELLY, Superintendent
National Capital Parks

Washington, D.C.
April 1, 1954

Your Washington

David W. Corson from A. Devaney, N.Y.

The Washington Monument

1. The Spirit of Washington

THERE is a legend that a ghostly figure stands alone in the tower of the Washington Monument as dawn rises above the Capitol.

It is a tall and awesome figure, to whom a visitor to royal courts once wrote: "I have known many, but you are the only one for whom I felt an awful reverence." The face is noble, selfless and intent. A rough military cloak hangs on his shoulders. He wears a weather-beaten, three-cornered hat.

To the schoolboys who will soon clatter noisily up the 898 steps of the monument, this is a familiar figure — George Washington, the Father of His Country. Now, so the legend goes, the lonely sentinel stares out the barred windows at the city of his choice, spread like jewels in a case below him.

There, guarded by the foothills of Maryland and Virginia, is the United States Government. It is powerful beyond any dream of the ragged army at Valley Forge, humane as man has learned to be, and the very democracy that Washington demanded against the cries that he become a king.

To the east, down the long, green Mall, the great dome of the Capitol is framed by the rising sun. There, men and women from the cities, towns and farms of a land that covers more than 3,000,000 square miles and holds 160,000,000 people, guide the government. Is there, perhaps, the shadow of a smile on the grave face of this ghostly figure? The spirit of Washington may recall his calm reply to one who complained of Congressional attacks upon his Administration:

"In government as free as ours, where the people are at liberty, and will express their sentiments (oftentimes imprudently, and, for want of information, sometimes unjustly), allowances must be made for occasional effervescences."

On either side of the Mall stand the storehouses of culture, treasures and heirlooms that the nation has collected. The figure in the tower can see the castle of the Smithsonian Institution, and the domes of the Natural History Building and the National Art Gallery.

To the left, in a grand sweep up Constitution Avenue, is a stately parade of buildings, with the clock tower of the Post Office cutting a wedge from the sky. The steady gaze of the watcher rests briefly on the Justice Department. One commandment of his Farewell Address is: "Respect for authority, compliance with laws, acquiescence in its measures, are fundamental duties of true Liberty. . . . The very idea of the power and right of the people to establish Government presupposes the duty of every individual to obey the established Government."

Beyond Constitution Avenue, as far as the eye can see, are stretched the temples of orderly government. On each desk within might be posted a slip of paper with Washington's warning of "the love of power, and proneness to abuse it, which predominates in the human heart."

Then, so the legend goes, the ghostly figure walks deliberately to each of the windows in the silent lookout. To the north, in that proud White House with a sloping lawn, sleeps a lonely man. Perhaps, even now, the President stirs restlessly in his sleep and calls out for a voice to advise him in his newest crisis. The spirit in the tower can offer this solace from his own soul:

"Of all the dispositions and habits which lead to political prosperity, Religion and Morality are indispensable. These are the great pillars of human happiness, the firm props in the duties of Men and Citizens."

Across the narrow lane from the White House stands a curious old building darkened by time. In the paneled rooms of this former State-

War-Navy Building, historic decisions were made. Here Lincoln somberly watched the path of Lee's march to Gettysburg and selected Grant to head the Union armies; here a belligerent Assistant Secretary of the Navy, Theodore Roosevelt, cried for war after the sinking of the *Maine;* here Woodrow Wilson heard the news that turned him slowly, painfully, away from his dream of peace; here Cordell Hull received word of Pearl Harbor; here, today, the National Security Council sets the nation's course in a troubled world.

To the west, there is breathless beauty. Far away, the drowsy mountains of Virginia slumber in the mists. Nearer, Arlington House, the hauntingly gracious home of the Lees, stands on the crest of a hill. The green slopes are marked with rows of white crosses. Below, Memorial Bridge spans the Potomac River, which winds gracefully until lost from sight.

At the river's edge, on the Washington side, the Lincoln Memorial rises unforgettably beyond the long reflecting pool. It is a single white flower on the edge of a green garden. The still waters of the pool mirror the long, straight marble shaft of the Washington Monument.

As the ghostly figure stands at this window, he stares long to the right. In the distance is Georgetown, the old colonial village whose homes heard many hopes and plans for the infant Republic. But this is not where his eyes linger; instead he looks at the cluster of large new buildings that are the State Department. Maybe his mind is full of his own words:

"Against the insidious wiles of foreign influence (I conjure you to believe me, fellow-citizens,) the jealousy of a free people ought to be constantly awake; since history and experience prove, that foreign influence is one of the most baneful foes of Republican government. But that jealousy, to be useful, must be impartial. . . .

"My politics are plain and simple. I think every nation has a right to establish that form of government under which it conceives it may live most happy; provided it infracts no right, or it is not dangerous to others, and that no governments ought to interfere with the internal concerns of another, except for the security of what is due to themselves."

There to the left, across the river, is the only weapon left when the diplomats fail — the vast sprawling Pentagon, home of the military commands. Deep in its caverns, hundreds of feet below ground to be safe from attack, a constant watch is kept on the world. A rattle of the teletype, a noisy telephone, warn of a flight of strange bombers over the Bering Sea. An order flashes to airfields across the world; whistling jet fighters and giant bombers are warmed up.

These frightening machines of modern destruction are unknown to George Washington, but he understands, as only a great leader can, that bravery and devotion are still an army's greatest prize. This figure in the tower remembers, too, his warning to future American governments: "They will avoid the necessity of those overgrown military establishments, which, under any form of government, are inauspicious to liberty, and which are to be regarded as particularly hostile to Republican Liberty."

The spirit of Washington, the legend goes, finally turns to the south. He looks wistfully past the Tidal Basin, the domed Jefferson Memorial, the slender finger of Hains Point, and even beyond the streets of Alexandria where he drilled the Virginia militia before they marched to Fort Duquesne and saw the lines of British regulars mowed down by snipers. He looks down the slow curves of the Potomac to the only real rest, Mount Vernon.

Now, with the light of day filling the tower, the vision vanishes. The sun fills the dark corners, welcoming the rush of visitors who will come when the doors below open at 9 o'clock. . . .

The monument to Washington grew very much like the nation he created. There were bursts of inspiration and energy, long stretches of indifference, and even a scandal that was more like an act of boyish pranksters than grown men.

Eight days after Washington's death, John Marshall, his devoted follower, asked Congress "that a marble monument be erected by the United States in the Capitol, at the city of Washington," in his honor.

Photo by Rideout — Courtesy National Park Service

But like the failure of the Continental Congress to supply Washington with men or supplies for a war of liberation, so the legislators argued days into months into years over designs and funds. The statue on horseback was altered to a granite and marble pyramid one hundred feet square at the base. Finally, years later, the House passed a bill giving two hundred thousand dollars for the pyramid. The Senate disagreed.

Much later, in 1832, the master orator Henry Clay used his talents in vain, crying out to the Senate, "As a monument, rear it, spend upon it what you will; make it durable as the pyramids, eternal as the mountains!"

After this, as a reprimand to a negligent Congress, citizens organized the Washington National Monument Society. School-children, church-goers, veterans, even sheriffs with donation cups, raised pennies, nickels and dimes. Leaflets pasted on cigar boxes and placed in ballot booths called lustily:

Every true lover of his country will contribute something this day, in aid of the

GREAT NATIONAL MONUMENT
TO
WASHINGTON

Have ready your donation, however small. The Contribution Box and the Ballot Box are this day side by side at every Poll in the United States.

A design for a National Pantheon was approved. It was to be a Greek temple 250 feet around and 100 feet high, with a shaft 600 feet high. A colossal statue of Washington would stand atop the temple. The drawings look like an edifice on the order of the Lincoln Memorial. Later this was modified to the clean straight shaft that towers today over all Washington.

The site actually had been picked by Washington as the ideal place for a dream close to his heart, a memorial to the men of the American Revolution. It was on a rise of land that could be seen alike by boats on the Potomac and coaches on the dusty woodland roads.

Forty-nine years after Marshall called for a monument, a huge July Fourth crowd stood patiently in the burning heat for the corner-stone rites. Orators poured out elegant phrases with a fervor that matched the sun's. One speaker who understood history said simply:

"His (Washington's) devotion to the ideal of the United States was the spark that kept it alive in the hours of darkness."

Six' years later the Washington Monument and the country were blighted by a kind of cancer that strikes new nations. It was an intolerance of "outsiders" on a vast, national scale — the "Know Nothing" movement. This was a secret, violently anti-foreign order. The name came from the members' pledge to do exactly as they were told, and reply "I know nothing" to all inquiries about the movement. The Know Nothings elected governors in seven states. A President, Millard Fillmore, was a member.

Many friendly nations sent blocks of stone to be a part of the Washington Monument. The gift of Greece, "mother of ancient liberty," was a block of white marble from the ruins of the Parthenon. The Vatican donated a marble block from the Temple of Concord.

One night in winter, a masked band of Know Nothings seized what they called "that marble block from Rome." It was taken from a shed on the monument grounds and apparently dumped in the Potomac.

In addition, the Know Nothings took over the records of the Monument Society, threw out the existing officers and put in their own. This vandalism, and the threat of the approaching War Between the States, almost stopped the collecting of funds. For nearly a quarter-century, the monument to Washington stood partly finished as a rebuke to his people. It was a broken sword, 153 feet tall.

When the war was done, the Government, by act of Congress, officially took over completion of the monument. But to those who look closely today there remains a sign of this neglect, perhaps as an eternal reprimand. The stone of the shaft in the original lower section has a slightly different shade. It was impossible to duplicate exactly the exact shade of white Maryland marble.

The nation watched the slow, steady progress. Each new stone in place erased a part of the shame. The monument stood clean and straight, 555 feet above ground, when the capstone was put in place on a December day. An account of the times relates: "The flag broke out in the wind and cannon thundered in salute."

But for the legendary spirit of George Washington, a greater hour was the 100th anniversary of the dedication. Then, on July 4, 1948, a modern President outlined America's place in the world:

"As the most powerful nation, we have assumed responsibilities which we must fulfill. We have fought the tremendous wars for freedom and liberty in the world. Our ambition is only for one thing, peace in the world and the welfare of the world as a whole. We have no territorial ambitions. We only ask for peace and justice."

Today, the Washington Monument is very dear to the people of this nation. It is as close to the dreams of those far from home as is the front porch and Main Street. Gabby Street, the Washington catcher and hero of boys, caught a baseball dropped from the monument. A Metropolitan Opera star sang from the tower to prove the carrying qualities of his voice. Couples have tried, without success, to be married in the monument. Scientists have gravely proclaimed that the shaft sinks one inch in fifty-four years.

On stormy nights, lightning strikes the rods on top, and echoes a roar. Women used to faint regularly in the elevator until a recording of a soothing male-voice description of the monument was played on the ups and downs. A Geiger counter detected precious uranium throughout the length of the shaft. An elderly couple, seventy-two and seventy-six, walked from Union Station to the monument, up the 898 steps, down again and back to the train.

Every night before closing, a guard walks carefully down the stairs to nab anyone who might try to stay the night on a dare. The monument weighs a giant 81,120 tons, but not even a wind of 145 miles an hour would send it crashing to the ground.

All this is Americana. But most of all, the true spirit of America crowds the door when the monument opens every morning at nine. Here is the United States, from Maine to California — husky high-school boys waving Confederate flags, an excited troop of Negro Girl Scouts, a quiet, white-haired couple on their thirtieth wedding anniversary, young Army trainees on their first leave. Most of them crowd into the huge elevator. As the door closes, the pleasant recorded voice from the loudspeaker begins, "Welcome, each of you, to the shrine . . ."

Those who climb the wide stairs, round and round the hollow shaft, have their own reward. It is a chance to look curiously at the blocks of stone sent from grateful people and nations. The inscriptions on some are written in Arabic, Greek and Mandarin. Here is the stout pledge of one state: "Under the auspices of heaven and the precepts of Washington, Kentucky will be the last to give up the Union." . . .

Over there is the "Gliosophic Society of Nassau Hall, N. J." . . . "a humble tribute from Two Disciples of Daguerre" . . . "the Sabbath School Children of Methodist Church of Philadelphia" . . . "Hibernian Society of Baltimore" . . . "Continental Guard of New Orleans" . . . "Employees of R. Norris and Sons Locomotive Works" . . . "the memory of the just is blesséd" . . .

Now, at last, here is the tower. To each in his own way, the views bring a strange sense of elation. The high-school boys talk a little louder. The newlyweds move closer together. The older visitors stand long in silent reverence. There, below, is all that Government should be — solid, orderly and with inspiring beauty. From here the noise and shouting below is lost.

This brings a new and deeply satisfying meaning to the words of Chateaubriand: "The name of Washington will spread with liberty from age to age!"

Photo by Abbie Rowe — Courtesy National Park Service

The Smithsonian

2. History's Treasure House

AN absurdly frail craft of bamboo, muslin and crude parts hangs in a queer old building on the Mall in Washington. Those who pass below on the worn stone floor stare up at it like some odd relic in an attic. A few exclaim in honest surprise: "Imagine anyone flying in *that!*"

Yet this frail craft is one of man's most terrifying creations, for it has robbed the world of space and time. It hovers over a military glory it has doomed forever — golden swords, cavalrymen's saddles, trim models of fighting frigates. A sign on the contraption reads: *The Original Wright Brothers Aeroplane, 1903.*

The plane seems like a huge and awkward kite, rigged with the kind of machinery that cartoonists attribute to mad inventors. Bicycle sprockets spin two propellers. The homemade engine might have been salvaged from a junk yard.

A wax-faced and mustached dummy, supposedly Orville Wright, lies prone on the wing, firmly grasping a steering bar. He is dressed like a young dandy at the turn of the century, in jaunty black cap, blue-serge suit, gold cuff links and white shirt with black tie. But the eyes are out of character. They look down on passers-by with a vague sadness, as though to say: "Forgive me. I only wanted to learn how to fly."

On a cold December afternoon in 1903, when wind drove the gulls shrieking along the beach at Kittyhawk, North Carolina, this "aeroplane" flew for twelve seconds. It lifted itself like a bird, rose straight and true into the air, and fell easily to earth. Thus, like shattering a

Photograph from the Smithsonian Institution

glass, the mystery of space was broken. Man's desire to escape into the heavens was appeased.

The Wright machine faces the visitor just inside the door of the, brick-and-tile Arts and Industries Building of the Smithsonian Institution. Outside, the ancient structure is pure rococo, remindful of an 1880 state fair. Inside it is a dimly lit and cluttered treasure house, smelling faintly of moth balls.

All about the Wright plane are signs of a civilization it has doomed. To the left, in a huge painting of a cavalry charge, the horses prance boldly, the men ride with a reckless grace that no twentieth-century jet pilot in a pressurized flying suit could attain. On the wall to the right, Union veterans march proudly, sun shining on their bayonets.

Exhibit cases below the "aeroplane" are filled with a lost pageantry ... the sword of General Winfield Scott, decorated with a miniature gold eagle atop the hilt ... an officer's belt sparkling with gold leaves ... a graceful flintlock pistol with delicately carved handle ... epaulets sagging with the weight of gold cord ... dainty silver spurs ... the romantic gray, red and gold uniform of a Confederate officer ... the feathered hat of the chief of the United States Army in 1828.

In the next room, the Hall of Navy History, the trim beauty of sailing ships and the sleekness of fast cruisers are lost beside the big model of a lumbering aircraft carrier, dominating the scene. This model stops the wide-eyed schoolboys. They pass by the frigate *Constitution* with an indifferent glance at its daring tale, and stop to count the miniature planes on the flat deck of the carrier.

And yet, for all the signs of past glories, a few steps more in this crowded storehouse prove that aviation could no more have been held back than the dawn.

Transportation Hall reveals the inexorable progress of man away from the power of his own legs. By the door is a creaking ox-cart with rough-hewn wooden wheels. Move ahead several generations and there is the elaborately decorated sedan chair, carried by husky servants while their haughty mistress swayed within.

The one-horse shay sits pertly in a long line of buggies. And further on the path of progress is the stylish high-wheeled racing bicycle; a cable car with varnished wooden seats; the "John Bull" locomotive; and the "horseless carriage" with steering bar that Elwood Haynes of Kokomo, Indiana, drove six miles on July 4, 1894.

The Smithsonian, now sprawled in four buildings on the Mall between the Washington Monument and the Capitol, owes its existence to the bitterness of an obscure British scientist, James Smithson, illegitimate son of the Duke of Northumberland. Denied his place in British society, he willed $500,000 to the United States, "to found at Washington, under the name of the Smithsonian Institution, an establishment for the increase and diffusion of knowledge among men." Its headquarters is a reproduction of an English castle — a towered stone-and-ivy-covered building with long, narrow windows.

Grouped about it are the Arts and Industries Building and the more conventional Natural History Building or, as it is known to thousands of visiting children, the "Old Bones" building. Beyond it is the Freer Gallery of Art, a temple to the talents of James McNeill Whistler.

Photograph from the Smithsonian Institution

Actually, that sanctuary for man, beast and peanut-vendors, the Washington Zoo, and the Mellon Art Gallery are also a part of the Smithsonian, as well as observatories spotted across the world for studying the heavens.

Altogether, the Smithsonian buildings are a maze of wonder where a dreamer can lose himself. The treasures are all about, like dandelions on a summer lawn.

There, under the shadow of the Wright plane, almost hidden by a row of exhibit cases, is a precious relic of freedom — the gallant, wind-torn Stars and Stripes. More than a century ago this flag gave new hope to America. A lawyer, captive on a British ship in Chesapeake Bay, saw it flying over Fort McHenry, and wrote with the power of emotion:

Oh, say can you see, by the dawn's early light, what so proudly we hailed at the twilight's last gleaming? . . . Oh, say does that Star

Spangled Banner yet wave, O'er the land of the free and the home of the brave?

A rare source of wonder for women lies around the corner from the Star-Spangled Banner, in another gloomy, crowded room. The feminine visitors move slowly, lingering at each exhibit case to exclaim at some bit of finery of the First Ladies of the White House. The wax model of Martha Washington is clothed in a salmon-pink gown, decorated with violets, buttercups, morning glories and arbutus, a shawl of priceless old lace, lace mitts and a white mob cap.

Photograph from the Smithsonian Institution

Gown Worn by Martha Washington

Dolly Madison, described by a reverent society writer as "unassuming dignity, sweetness and grace," stands in an overdress of yellow satin, a white petticoat of wild rose, cherry blossom and forget-me-not design, and a turban. The beautiful Harriet Lane Johnston, niece of James Buchanan, with lace lightly brushing her lovely neck and shoulders, wears a sweeping white moiré taffeta with tight bodice and low neck. Unhappy Mary Todd Lincoln displays a velvet gown of her favorite color, royal purple, with sleeves of white lace and a bouquet of pansies. . . .

But forget this glimpse of the near past by a quick walk across the width of the grassy Mall, and enter a realm of the long, long ago — the Natural History Building. The visitors stand before such a sight as a tableau of two hundred million years ago, where a fossil bed on exhibit tells a tragic tale.

Giant amphibians — huge, lizard-like creatures living in the swamps and ponds of a world of mountains, seas and lush jungles — were visited with the curse of drought. The pools dried up into dry, cracking earth. The amphibians, dying, choking, starving, fought to the edge of a remaining pool and died there. This happened two hundred million years ago in what is now New Mexico.

Move on in time to another room where Man enters the world. Case after case of primitive people at work and play, dressed in the bright colors they loved . . . Indians, stoic and proud with dignity . . . happy, dark-eyed Igorots returning from the hunt . . . slim, black Veddas of Ceylon. Among all these savages there is none of the furrowed brow, the frantic look, seen in any crowd of today. What has civilization done to Man?

Other strange questions arise. Over here are fragments of meteorites, their hard black surfaces pitted by violent heat created in flight through the earth's atmosphere. They flamed across the skies from outer space and fell on inaccessible mountain slopes and deserts. What hand of Providence kept them from the cities of men?

A scientist might find a clue to an ancient mystery — how far is Man from beast — in another exhibit. This was timidly placed in the Smithsonian after much soul-searching by the directors.

The exhibit is of a primitive tribe in Ecuador who, by their faces, are simple, undesigning folk. Their claim to fame is a curious ritual — shrinking the heads of their enemies — much as a more civilized people mount the heads of deer shot in sport.

The savage trophies are small, about the size of a fist, with leathery faces and long, glossy strands of hair. The demand for them by white explorers who enter the jungles is so great that a brisk business of manufacturing counterfeits flourishes among the savages.

But there is still another world in the Smithsonian, a world where all is beauty — the Freer Gallery. Room after room shows the intimate, discerning line — the poetry of color, the mystery of light — all products of Whistler's genius. He understood, as only a man and lover can, the grace of a feminine figure.

In every corner of the Smithsonian is some exhibit to inspire the wonder of every visitor. Not only in America but through the world the name Smithsonian has come to mean knowledge.

Not long ago, a writer inquired: "Please send me all the information on the end of the world."

Actually, the Smithsonian has no interest in such morbid topics as catastrophe and death. It is a vast and wonderful treasure house of life and progress. A visitor moving through its buildings can trace the beginnings of life when the mists about the earth cooled. Then he can go on to learn the life and habits of every age.

If anything is featured in these halls, it is the adventure and daring of man. Somehow that seems fitting for a museum owned by the American people.

Lincoln Memorial

3. Where Lincoln Lives

THIS year, some two million Americans will visit a hallowed shrine of freedom by the river's edge in Washington. It stands serene and alone on a rise of land where ninety years ago a lonely man brooded upon the fate of the Union.

Abraham Lincoln came often to the bank of the slow-moving Potomac that divided a nation. Often the distant thundering of cannon was mingled with the cheerful song of birds. On Lincoln's side lay the Union; on the hill across stood the one-time mansion of the Confederacy's Robert E. Lee.

As Lincoln looked thoughtfully at the green Virginia hills, he must have recalled the sorrowing words of his first Inaugural Address: "We are not enemies, but friends. We must not be enemies. Though passion may have strained, it must not break our bonds of affection . . ."

In 1867, two years after Lincoln's death, Congress began the ponderous march toward a memorial on this rise of land where he had dreamed of peace and unity. But for forty-six years, men could not agree on the kind of tribute a grateful nation should erect. In one debate a Senator argued:

"I believe that a fitting memorial should take a form more pronounced than the erection of a monument in rivalry with the Washington Monument. A statue or a corner in a park will be no memorial to him."

He favored, as did many of his colleagues, a "Lincoln Way" — a highway from Washington to Gettysburg to rival the Appian Way

Winston Pote, A. Devaney, Inc., N.Y.

of ancient Rome. But another Senator said: "A memorial should be so big that the people will see it when they enter Washington . . ."

Finally, the Lincoln Memorial Commission asked the advice of Henry Bacon, noted architect. He favored a Greek temple, and found a partisan in the Senate to declare: "Few remnants of the architecture of Greece have survived, yet we stand in wonder before those that remain twenty centuries after their day."

The next issue was the site. Many wanted it to be a part of the Capitol grounds. Only a few thought of the river's edge where Lincoln had found faith to carry him through a host of trials. They were supported by the President's secretary and biographer, John Hay, who urged that the memorial be located on the axis of the celebrated Washington Plan, in line with the Capitol and the Washington Monument.

"His monument should stand alone," said Hay, "remote from the business and turmoil of the city, isolated, distinguished and serene."

So here was placed the memorial, looking over Washington from the river's edge like a guardian angel. It would be a Greek temple of shining white marble, rising from the deep green foliage of Potomac Park. It would enshrine a single, unforgettable figure of Lincoln.

Daniel Chester French, who had re-created the great epics of our history in such statues as "The Minute Man," was chosen as sculptor. For half a century, artists had been striving to capture Lincoln's qualities in oils and stone. This new figure, French decided, must be the greatest and most understanding.

The sculptor's models were a life mask of Lincoln and plaster copies of his hands. For six years, French worked to create truth and beauty out of clay. The task was difficult, for Lincoln had had an elusive and mystic character: his face was both majestic and homely, tender and yet stern with purpose. And always, his hands showed an immense moral strength.

Once, to get a sense of relaxed strength in Lincoln's right hand, French put his own hand in various positions. When he found the exact expression, the fingers loosely placed on the arm of a chair, the sculptor had his hand cast in plaster. Then he studied the cast as he worked painstakingly on the model.

When finally the white marble was carved into the likeness of Lincoln and placed in the temple against a limestone wall and above a pink marble floor, French came to view the statue. The sculptor was shocked: Lincoln was gaunt and seemed misshapen. Light from the Memorial's open side struck the gleaming floor and reflected a ghastly brilliance on the figure.

The problem was solved by placing a series of slatted panels in the ceiling with floodlights behind them, and a thick coating of beeswax on the marble slabs. This gave a radiant, translucent glow to the towering statue.

On Memorial Day, 1922, the Lincoln Memorial was turned over to the American people with simple ceremonies. It was a gentle afternoon of spring, and the glittering Potomac was a background

for the eulogies addressed to the great crowd. Edwin Markham read his stirring poem in honor of the martyred President:

> *And when he fell in whirlwind, he went down*
> *As when a lordly cedar, green with boughs,*
> *Goes down with a great shout upon the hills,*
> *And leaves a lonesome place against the sky.*

Since that day, the memorial has become America's most hallowed shrine. More visitors reverently climb its sweeping steps than those of any other monument in the United States. It has a mood and personality all its own, as though Lincoln were sitting there, deep in thought. Even youthful students who clatter noisily from buses lower their voices and take off their hats lest they disturb his spirit.

Many older visitors cry, unashamed. Not too long ago, aged veterans of the Grand Army of the Republic would painfully climb the steps and kneel in prayer before their idol. Today, letters of affection and appeal in scrawled handwriting are still addressed to "A. Lincoln, The Lincoln Memorial, Washington, D.C."

The memorial faithfully carries out the plea of John Hay that it "stand alone, remote from the business and turmoil of the city, isolated, distinguished and serene." The temple of pure white marble rises majestically on a knoll near the river. The steps incline upward to huge fluted columns, twelve on the east and west sides, six on the north and south sides — one for each of the thirty-six States of the Republic at the time of Lincoln's death. Surrounded by deep green boxwood, the memorial faces east, across the long and graceful reflecting pool, to the spiring Washington Monument.

Through the open side, a seated Lincoln beholds a sight beyond mortal vision. Above his seated figure is inscribed in stone:

> *In This Temple*
> *As In the Hearts of the People*
> *For Whom He Saved the Union*
> *The Memory of Abraham Lincoln*
> *Is Enshrined Forever.*

The long and rugged face, alive in marble, is strong and kindly. A lock of unruly hair falls over Lincoln's massive and careworn forehead. The rough beard follows the slanting lines of his face inward and over his chin. His deep-set eyes are lonely; the nose is positive, the underlip stubborn.

His left hand is clenched tightly on the arm of the President's bench. The knuckles stand out sharply. The right hand grasps the edge of the bench with sensitive fingers.

On either side of the central chamber, beyond Ionic columns, are smaller chambers, with sweeping murals on two walls. On one side is the Angel of Truth, joining the hands of North and South. Below, the Second Inaugural Address is cut in stone, in letters a foot high: ". . . With malice toward none; with charity for all; with firmness in the right, as God gives us to see the right, let us strive on to finish the work we are in; to build up the Nation's wounds; to care for him who shall have borne the battle, and for his widow and his orphan, to do all which may achieve and cherish a just and lasting peace among ourselves and with all nations."

On the south wall, the Angel of Truth is freeing a slave. Below are imperishable words from the Gettysburg Address:

"Four score and seven years ago our fathers brought forth on this continent a new nation conceived in liberty and dedicated to the proposition that all men are created equal . . . That we here highly resolve that these dead shall not have died in vain — that this nation under God shall have a new birth of freedom — and that government of the people, by the people, for the people, shall not perish from the earth."

The spirit of a lonely man, who stood on a rise of land overlooking the Potomac and pondered the fate of the Union, is surely alive in that temple. Today, as yesterday, the simple faith and wisdom of Abraham Lincoln offers a guide to all Americans as they seek to weather the storms that crash around our modern world.

Photo by Abbie Rowe — Courtesy National Park Service

The White House

4. The House of Hope

AN elderly stranger stood outside the iron picket fence and looked at the proud white mansion beyond. The pillared house gleamed in the sun like moonlight on the water. An autumn wind tore bright leaves from graceful old elms and tossed them recklessly over the broad lawn.

At their post inside the West Gate, two uniformed White House guards regarded the stranger curiously. They decided he was no casual tourist, nor an angry-eyed fanatic who might demand entrance.

The sergeant began a friendly conversation as gray squirrels scampered at his feet. The stranger explained: "I have been thinking how much the President needs hope. I am an old man and no longer need mine. I was trying to give my hope to him."

The sergeant was wise and observing, and he understood. He had seen Presidents at the end of the day almost numb with care. The guard spoke gravely: "I am sure the President will be grateful. The White House needs hope. God help our country if it goes long without it. You might call this, sir, the 'House of Hope. . . .'"

The White House was built on the hopes that all who ruled from here would love liberty as much as life itself. The hope of its first tenant, John Adams, was ordered inscribed above the fireplace of the State Dining Room by Franklin Roosevelt, more than a century later: "I pray Heaven to bestow the best of blessings on this House and all that shall hereafter inhabit it. May none but honest and wise men ever rule under this roof."

Photograph from the Library of Congress

The hope of Abraham Lincoln for a nation united still walks the upstairs halls in long, patient strides on lonely nights. The hope of Woodrow Wilson for world peace lingers in the sick room where he said spiritedly, "Better a thousand times go down fighting than to dip your colors to a dishonorable compromise." The hope of Presidents brought to life in hundreds of despairing, sleepless nights lives within the proud white walls.

Mrs. Eleanor Roosevelt often told visitors how these hopes dwell in the White House. "You cannot live there and not feel the atmosphere of solemn responsibility," she said. And President Harry S. Truman believed he was guided, regardless of his own inclinations, by the hopes and wisdom of the past lords of this mansion.

The United States itself was little more than a hope when the cornerstone of the White House was laid in 1792. Washington was a swampy village of 3200. The Federal Government was all of 128 persons. In this setting, the President's house seemed, even to such a traveled man as Thomas Jefferson, as "big enough for two emperors, one Pope and the Grand Lama."

When President Adams moved in, water was carried by hand from a spring half a mile away. The White House was on a knoll looking southward to the Potomac River, and north, to peacefully grazing cows. There were no bathrooms in the mansion. Mrs. Adams wrote resignedly, "We had not the least fence, yard or other convenience without, and the great unfinished audience room (the magnificent East Room of today), I made a drying room of. Nor were there enough 'lusters' or lamps, so candles were stuck here and there for light."

The British contemptuously burned the White House in the late summer of 1814. After this act of vengeance, a mighty storm struck the city. Of the burned remains, one Washington observer wrote sadly: "In the President's House not an inch, but it's crak'd and blacken'd walls remain'd. That scene which when I last visited it was so splendid, throng'd with the great, the gay, the ambitious placeman, the patriotic heroes, was now nothing but ashes. Oh, vanity of human hopes!"

This writer failed to understand that our young nation was filled with the same hope that gave settlers the heart to rebuild their cabins after Indian raids. The President's house was carefully restored and painted white. The American people named it forever the "White House."

A visitor in the mid-nineteenth century described the restored mansion: "It resembles the country seat of an English nobleman in architecture and size. The interior is well disposed and possesses one superb reception room and two oval drawing rooms of very beautiful proportions. There is inequality in the furniture of the whole house, owing to the unwillingness and piecemeal manner in which Congress votes any moneys for its decoration."

With the growth and change of the new nation, the White House changed, too. The candles were replaced by gas lights in the great chandeliers, then electricity. The huge timbers were bored into, sawed and split to make room for new ways of living.

Photo by Abbie Rowe — Courtesy National Park Service

But finally, in 1948, the underpinnings and rafters of the proud mansion showed the ravages of time. The chandeliers swayed; the floor of the President's study trembled.

Some architects and builders believed the White House should be razed, every stone and timber pulled down, and a complete new mansion and office building erected. Others asked, where would the memories of Jefferson, Jackson, Lincoln rest if the White House were torn down? This was more than a building of stone and steel and wood. It was American history and hopes.

Thus, a most unusual feat was undertaken — the affectionate and painstaking demolition of the White House interior. To the tourist staring through the picket fence on Pennsylvania Avenue, the proud white mansion was the same. But within, like a jeweler removing a precious stone from its mounting, craftsmen cut out and put away for restoration the carved woodwork, the decorations and even the moldings.

Today, the White House stands more magnificent and enduring than ever. History still lives with it in the long Lincoln bed, the Minerva clock, the Roosevelt tiles, and a hundred other signs of glory.

The White House is many places in one. To most Americans, it is a shrine, a palace of democracy. The man who rules from here was chosen by them directly. Never was this mood stronger than when the people swarmed over the White House for their champion, Andrew Jackson, on his Inaugural Day. A horrified Washington aristocrat wrote: "The Majesty of the People had disappeared, and a rabble, a mob, scrabbling, fighting, romping, what a pity, what a pity! The President was nearly pressed to death, almost suffocated and torn to pieces by the people in their eagerness to shake hands with Old Hickory."

Today the American people come by the thousands every morning to view the rooms where history may be made that night. Their manner is one of reverence. The tourists walk through a patio where they can see neat gardens lining the walk to the south. Up the stairs, a stately grandfather clock gravely regards them. Beyond this is the East Room, whose grandeur brings gasps of surprise.

The long gold and white room is a chamber of laughter and tears and solemnity. Gay parties and weddings have been held below the famous chandeliers of 5000 sparkling pieces of crystal. Lincoln stood here, patiently shaking hands with well-wishers. Suddenly one far down the line cried out: "Mr. President, in my State they say that the welfare of the nation depends on God and Abraham Lincoln."

The tall and homely Lincoln answered wryly: "My friend, you are half right."

In the shadow of America's most treasured portrait, the full-length Stuart painting of Washington which Dolly Madison cut from the frame just before the British set fire to the White House, hushed lines of mourners have moved past the bodies of three Presidents. In this room the new President traditionally swears in his staff. But this is no museum of the past. Twelve hours after the tourists stare with awe at the Rouge Antique mantels, the President may lean an elbow on the veined red marble and discuss a major move with his Secretary of State.

The visitors pass curiously through the startlingly vivid Green, Red and Blue Rooms with satin walls. Herbert Hoover liked to dine on the South Portico just outside the Blue Room, because of the inspiration which he gained from viewing the Washington Monument. During his last year in office, Hoover pointed to the monument and told a dinner guest, "This, apparently, is the only stable thing in my Administration."

During World War II his successor, Franklin Roosevelt, used the Red Room as a map room. He would be wheeled through the splendor of the State Dining Room into the red and white chamber with the famous gilt bronze clock. There he would pore over global maps, planning an action in some far distant area.

The State Dining Room holds tourists for many minutes. This is an appropriate place for history . . . soft walls and lights, silver chandeliers, and a thoughtful portrait of Lincoln over the majestic black marble mantel. It is easy to imagine a President posing a great issue to his guests in the candlelight.

To the north is the simple, dignified and warm Entrance Hall. The President's guests arrive in this white marble lobby, and here he bids them farewell. One recent guest tells of a haunting experience in this Hall: "President Eisenhower had been so gay and charming at dinner, it was hard to remember he had cares. As we were leaving, on the steps of the North Portico, I turned back to look at the President standing there alone. The change was startling. He looked as though the weight of the world had fallen on him. I will never forget his face at that moment."

On the ground floor below is a room alive with greatness. This is the President's library, where he can borrow hope and wisdom from the printed word. The wood wainscot is of timbers from the old White House. The Delft tiles around the fireplace were designed by Franklin Roosevelt and show scenes from the life of a President.

On the second floor, where the Presidential family lives, the

Lincoln Room is a quiet shrine. The long extra-length bed is the one in which he tossed through the unhappy nights. The spirit of Lincoln lives, too, in the room where official visitors wait their turn. The spirit is in a painting of Lincoln and his advisors, called "The Peace Makers," often regarded as his best likeness.

The lobby in the West or office wing is usually filled with reporters, photographers' gear, friendly guards and impatient visitors. A unique table with steers' heads carved into the legs fills the center of the room.

Beyond and to the left, the President's oval office is bright and cheerful. Behind his desk the long windows look out on a rich rose garden. Before him is a world globe. This room, small compared to the awesome throne rooms of some Cabinet members, is a sanctuary. Here a President can be himself, away from the demanding stare of cameras, the lure of microphones, and a crowd quick to catch any weakness. Here he can afford to be humble.

President Truman would walk to the globe many times a day, look at it searchingly — as if here might miraculously appear the solution to some problem — and then say, almost to himself, "God hope that we can find peace!"

The White House has its warm side as the home of Presidents and their families. Jefferson, as any unreconstructed tinkerer, created gadgets. One of them was a rotating clothes hanger he installed in his closets. Jefferson also drew up plans for the North Portico, and introduced ice cream to the United States at White House dinners.

John Quincy Adams puttered among the shrubs and trees he planted on the lawns, raised silkworms and played billiards. Andrew Jackson liked to sit before a blazing fire in a long, loose coat, smoking a pipe and surrounded by young nieces and nephews. Lincoln's two sons, Willie and Tad, tore through the mansion as lively boys will. Teddy Roosevelt's five children made the White House their personal playground. Calvin Coolidge had his mechanical horse for exercise, and Franklin Roosevelt had his swimming pool for relaxation. Dwight Eisenhower practiced golf on the south lawn.

Most of all, though, the White House is a place of decision, illustrated by a sign which sat on Truman's desk, "The Buck Stops Here." This explains the lesson every President must learn — that the decisions that crowd in upon him must be made alone. That is why the White House, behind the gay exterior, is such a sad place, or, as William Howard Taft told Woodrow Wilson, "I am glad to be going — this is the lonesomest place in the world."

This explains why Lincoln, in a strange way, is the patron saint of this mansion. When peace came, Lincoln sat at his White House desk and wrote a hope that, more than anything else, slowly reknitted the nation: "With malice toward none, with charity for all, with firmness in the right as God gives us to see the right, let us strive to finish the work we are in."

Almost every corner of the mansion is alive with some memory of Lincoln. Some of the old Negro servants swear they have seen his ghost, tall, lonely, sad, pacing the halls on nights when the White House is oppressive with decisions in the making. One secretary, an intelligent woman, told of being frightened by the ghost sitting on his bed in the "Lincoln Room" upstairs, pulling on his boots.

Every President since Lincoln has felt a strange kinship with him. They, too, have learned how a President must stand alone, rebuffed by Congress, reviled by coarse voices, powerless to hold together a quarreling Cabinet, and faced with decisions that change the destiny of a world.

John Quincy Adams made a notation in his diary that gives this mood. Adams lost control of Congress in mid-term, because he had the courage to propose a constructive but momentarily unpopular program. Many nights, sleep deserted him and he took long walks before dawn. On January first of his last year, Adams wrote: "This year begins in gloom. The dawn was overcast, and, as I began to write, my shaded lamp went out. The notice of so trivial an incident may serve but to mark the temper of my mind."

Elihu Root described the spirit of his friend Chester A. Arthur: "He was alone. He was bowed down by the weight of fearful responsibility and crushed to earth by the feeling, exaggerated but not unfounded, that he took up his heavy burden surrounded by dislike, suspicion, distrust and condemnation. Deep and settled melancholy possessed him; almost despair overwhelmed him . . . . "

From these trials and sadnesses, from the hopes that pierce the gloom have emerged from the White House great principles of the American way of life. The noisy scratching of Andrew Jackson's pen produced an eternal idea: "Every man is entitled to protection by law. When laws undertake to make the rich richer and the potent more powerful . . . the humble members of society have a right to complain of the injustice of their government."

Wilson pounded out on an old typewriter a declaration of American foreign policy: "We will not choose the path of submission," and, "peace without vengeance . . . self-determination for the little peoples."

Wilson's dream was defeated, but this hope was recreated a generation later when Franklin Roosevelt and Winston Churchill sat together in the quiet library and wrote the "Declaration of the United Nations." It is no wonder that with all this greatness alive in the White House, one servant thoughtfully advised an overnight guest: "You think someone is knocking on your door in the middle of the night. But don't pay it no mind. Nobody will be there — nobody you can see."

HERE RESTS IN
HONORED GLORY
AN AMERICAN
SOLDIER
KNOWN BUT TO GOD

Photo by Abbie Rowe — Courtesy National Park Service

Tomb of the Unknown Soldier

5. "Here Rests in Honored Glory ..."

A N American soldier lies sleeping forever beside a peaceful winding road across the Potomac River from the bustle and hubbub of Washington.

The road begins with a gentle slope at the end of busy Memorial Bridge. To the left, traffic rushes impatiently toward the Pentagon, a vast, odd-shaped bulding amid a sea of parked cars. Straight ahead, sorrowing and reverent Americans drive through heavy gates swung open to admit them to Arlington National Cemetery.

On a recent afternoon, when the sun made bright stars of light on the Potomac, a gray coupé from Nebraska left the traffic behind. It took the winding road and moved slowly into a thickening silence.

New sounds came forth like objects gradually focusing in a darkened room. There was the regular breathing of a light wind through trees, and the faraway song of birds. All else except an occasional airplane roar was a dim murmur, as the city began to move homeward in the late afternoon.

The trees sighing on the hillside gave the mood of peace. They were sturdy and tolerant oaks; elms with their limbs lifted as in prayer; plaintive willows; and shapely firs.

Off the road on either side, white tombstones stood in rows on the green hills like patient sentinels. At one unguarded spot gravediggers were piling red Virginia clay into two neat mounds. Another soldier soon would lie in undisturbed slumber.

Photo by Abbie Rowe — Courtesy National Park Service

The only other cars on the road were a black hearse and a lonely limousine behind. An elderly man and woman sat in the rear seat. The tombstones were so close to the road now that the names stood out clearly. "Booth . . . Matthews . . . Dale . . . Brown."

The Nebraska coupé pulled into the parking space below the amphitheater. A heavy man got out awkwardly. He wore a leather jacket and his trousers flapped in the breeze. He held the door open for his wife. She was smaller and neater and dressed in black. They were both young.

They stood without talking and looked up the hill. The first crimson of sunset burned the sky. Shadows slipped across the white columns of the amphitheater. But strangely, the Tomb of the Unknown Soldier was untouched. It was a dazzling brilliance of marble, a Sir Galahad among the Knights.

A uniformed sentry stood motionless to one side of the Tomb. His rifle lay against his shoulder. The sun caught a shining surface of the bayonet and flashed it far beyond. Behind him, an American flag fluttered at half-staff.

The sentry turned with a hard click of his heels. He paced to the sentry box on the north in easy, measured tread. His feet made only a soft padding noise on the narrow rubber catwalk. He stopped and turned, to face again the city across the river.

The man and woman from Nebraska walked slowly up the steps. At the top they halted reverently before the Tomb. He took off his hat and a stray gust ruffled his hair. She held his hand tightly and read the singing words:

> HERE RESTS IN
> HONORED GLORY
> AN AMERICAN
> SOLDIER
> KNOWN BUT TO GOD

The sentry passed them twice before the quiet, nameless mood was broken by the friendly voice of a sight-seeing guide. The wiry man shepherding a small party said: "I'd recommend that you folks stay for the changing of the guard. It'll be in a few minutes. Mighty impressive! Makes you feel there'll always be American men, like that boy there, guarding the things we love."

All of them looked at the sentry more carefully. Suddenly he was more than a trim figure in khaki uniform and white gloves.

The woman from Nebraska said in surprise: "Why, George, he looks like the Albright boy at the drugstore back home!"

A white-haired ex-officer, a colonel with a black mourning band on his sleeve, said proudly: "He's a good soldier."

The seven boys on their way to an Army base for training watched the sentry curiously. The one with a huge "S" on his sweater said half-enviously, "Do you suppose we'll look like that, Ed, after our basic?"

The guide noticed the Nebraska couple and said in a neighborly tone: "Where are you folks from?"

The man answered. "Up near Scottsbluff, in Nebraska."

Photo by Abbie Rowe — Courtesy National Park Service

His wife said impulsively: "I like to think . . ." But she stopped, embarrassed. The guide and the colonel looked at her kindly. Thus encouraged, she said shyly, "I like to think the Unknown Soldier might be my brother. This is his birthday. He died eight years ago."

The draftees moved restlessly, a little ill at ease with death so personal and close at hand. The officer knew the Unknown Soldier had fallen in World War I, but he said in quiet dignity: "All of us who have lost a soldier are sure that he lies buried here."

From the rear, a voice spoke a sharp command. Two pairs of heels came clicking smartly down the walk. A corporal escorted the new sentry to the south post. The old guard stood to the north.

These were different faces — one blue-eyed and clean-cut beneath the brim of his cap, another square and determined, the third long with a sharp chin. They were all very young and serious, for this was a man's business.

The three boys stood at attention. The corporal was directly in front of the Tomb with his hand raised in salute, the sentries at his

Photo by Abbie Rowe — Courtesy National Park Service

sides. They looked out over this peaceful hill that was theirs to guard. Their straight backs and shoulders gave a calm assurance.

This moment put fresh strength into each uneasy heart. The seven draftees on the rim of a new and uncertain life felt a nobility they did not know before. The colonel discovered again that American men are worthy of fallen heroes. The woman from Nebraska understood now that her brother was guarded by the devotion of a nation.

The moment was not long. The corporal dropped his salute, and the privates brought their rifles to "Right Shoulder Arms!" with brisk slaps on leather slings. The corporal and the retiring sentry marched off and vanished. The lone soldier halted, turned, and paced the worn catwalk.

The sight-seeing guide remarked, "That's all, folks. They'll be closing the gates now."

The Nebraska man called "Good luck, boys!" to the draftees. His wife and the colonel shook hands. The cars began to move down the winding road.

Those who looked back saw the Tomb framed in the last glory of the setting sun. It was white and pure against a crimson sky. The sentry, alone with his trust, stood straight and tall.

In his keeping lay the Soldier who, though unknown, symbolizes the honored dead of a nation — a great nation that believes in peace and yet is always ready to fight for liberty and freedom.

Garden at Mount Vernon

6. Mount Vernon: Symbol of Faith

D URING these 1950's, almost two centuries after the signing of our Declaration of Independence, Americans might well take time to contemplate a serene and quiet Virginia hilltop not far from Washington, D.C.

Close by the Potomac's edge, a white mansion with red-shingled roof and windowed cupola looks out over trim gardens and small buildings that reach to distant woods. Here the peaceful acres of Mount Vernon symbolize a spirit that created our nation.

A tall man with commanding presence stands alone in the freshness of dawn. Early sunlight sifts through the mist over the river, making slender shadows of the trees on the sloping lawn, glowing warmly on the white-brick porch where he stands. A clean smell of growing things fills the air.

The dawn softens George Washington's face — molded into straight lines by wars, privation and the hard birth of a nation. Now the wide, stern lips, the eyes that look beyond men, greet the day with a strange warmth.

Washington treasures this moment. No matter what the bitterness of yesterday, a wakening sun brings new hope. Standing quietly in the doorway of Mount Vernon, he thinks of the words he will write to a friend: "A man's best reward is his freedom and his own acres of land. They are the bed and the seed for a good life. They now belong to all in America. I pray every man gains the same happiness I have from these gifts . . . I can truly say I had rather be at Mount Vernon with a friend or two about me, than to be attended at the seat of government by the representatives of every power in Europe."

The lane leading to Mount Vernon is shielded by woods and quiet. The road opens suddenly on a broad lawn and well-kept hedges. Beyond the wooden gates and along the gravel path is a land symbolic of a just and orderly mind.

Between the walls of hedge as high as a man's head, the crew works cheerfully under the spring sun. Workmen in knee breeches and rough coats dig into the dark soil at exact, marked intervals.

Looking up, Washington sees his wife entering the garden. "Now we have all the berries needed for the kitchen," he says with pride. "In the first row there will be currants, the next raspberries, then gooseberries, and strawberries."

Martha Washington smiles at his eagerness and asks, "Where will you place the new cistern?"

"I have read that cisterns must conform to the old custom of exposing water to sunlight and air. This softens the water and makes it a proper drink for growing plants. So I will place the cistern in the center." Then he adds, "A garden must be planned as carefully as a man's life."

On either side of Mount Vernon lie rolling pastures. The living area is shielded by stone walls, draped with ivy.

In the Mansion House hall hangs a dramatic memento of freedom — the key to the French Bastille. Beyond the music room with its harpsichord is the green-walled banquet hall, where the man who rejected a crown sat with his guests of an evening. The visitors smoked their long pipes, drank clear wine and talked of tomorrow. The times were stern, enemies threatened from without, but here people could converse with deliberation.

The men talk eagerly. Each is characteristic in his own way — the thin and aristocratic nose of one, another's eloquent, deep-set eyes, the lofty forehead of a third, and a fourth's sensitive hands. But it is the host, straight-backed, serious, listening, who holds the focus.

There in one corner is the ancient globe he fingered to trace the course of British warships. His sword rests in another corner. Books that gave him knowledge of science and war and mankind fill the shelves.

On this last day of his life, Washington read until 9 o'clock, his usual hour of retiring. He awoke in the night seriously ill, but remained silent for fear of disturbing his wife. By morning he was ebbing fast, and that evening he died.

No one can say what was on Washington's mind those last hours. But he must have known that but for the serenity of Mount Vernon, this nation might have fallen.

Great decisions that demanded courage, intelligence and faith were bred on that Virginia hilltop — decisions to stand through the terrible winter at Valley Forge, to refuse the popular cry to become a king, to build instead a workable democracy for the American people.

Washington still rests at Mount Vernon among the cedars, oaks and elms that he loved. The brick crypt, grown over with ivy, stands on the edge of a wood whose floor is a thick carpet of myrtle. Engraved in stone are words of hope and consolation for all:

"I am the resurrection and the life, saith the Lord, he that believeth in Me, though he were dead, yet shall he live and whosoever liveth and believeth in Me shall never die."

Drawing Room of the Lee Mansion

7. The Master of Arlington

A WHITE-PILLARED mansion stands proud and alone on a hill-crest facing Washington. This was the home of a truly great man given to a people in their time of trial — Robert E. Lee.

He was a saint to his soldiers and a Christian who bore defeat with humility. Without him, our land today might be threatened by constant civil war. And Arlington, instead of being a Virginia shrine, might be a fortress.

As it is, the spirit of Lee still lingers in the quiet rooms and across the sloping lawns. A visit to Arlington House enables one to understand the man who wrote in the midst of a tragic war: "What a beautiful world God has given us! What a shame that men endowed with reason and knowledge should mar His gifts!"

The columned mansion, designed with simplicity and purity, is surrounded by yellow jasmine. Ivy climbs a massive oak: a giant cedar shadows the doorway. And just below, on the lawn reaching toward the broad Potomac, are rows of white tombstones which mark the resting place of America's honored dead.

Although Arlington House is so intimately associated with Lee that it is known as the "Lee Mansion," the home was built by his father-in-law, George Washington Park Curtis, foster son of the first President. Curtis obtained the services of an Irish architect who had come to Washington to design the Capitol, and Arlington House is an integrated combination of Greek temple and graceful Colonial mansion.

Here at Arlington, handsome Lieutenant Lee, not long out of

West Point, married Mary Anne Randolph Curtis; here six of his children were born; and here he spent his happiest moments and made his greatest decisions.

For a time, the North tried to wipe out the memory of Lee at Arlington. The vast grounds were converted into a cemetery for the Union dead, and is known today as Arlington National Cemetery, site of the Tomb of the Unknown Soldier. And yet, sixty-seven years after the Civil War began, the United States restored the mansion as a memorial to Lee.

Today, Arlington House is alive with personality. There is none of the musty quality of a museum asleep with its past, none of the haughtiness of a Georgetown mansion. The Lees regarded their home as in the country, where they could rear their daughters unspoiled by the giddy whirl of Washington or Richmond.

In the rear yard, the sturdy brick slave quarters, far superior to the cabins of many Southern white settlers, reflect Lee's own thoughts: "In this enlightened age, there are few but will acknowledge that slavery is a moral and political evil in any country."

Within Arlington House there is a feeling that the host has momentarily excused himself and invited you to make yourself at home. A chess board with men laid out beckons the guest to a game of matching wits. Upstairs, well-worn toys lie on the playroom floor. In the state dining room hangs a crystal chandelier with places for 36 candles. But these are placed alone like a single fire at night, not crowded in with a profusion of extravagant decorations.

In almost every room there is one item to stir the memory. In Lee's study is a prophetic painting, the British surrender to Washington at Yorktown. Perhaps that familiar scene came back to Lee at Appomattox, when he said in despair: "There is nothing left, but to go to General Grant, and I would rather die a thousand deaths!"

The decision whose inexorable end came at Appomattox was made by Lee at Arlington in those hours after midnight when a man's thoughts become as real as human touch. The date was April 20, 1861.

Photo by Abbie Rowe — Courtesy National Park Service

Lee had been recalled to Washington by his admirer and patron, General Winfield Scott, and arrived at Arlington on March 1. All during this month, events moved passionately and relentlessly. The Confederate States set up their secession capital at Montgomery, Alabama. Abraham Lincoln was inaugurated President. Fort Sumter was besieged and surrendered to the Confederacy. Lincoln called for an army of volunteers.

During these days when the shadow of civil war darkened, a conflict grew in Lee's mind. He was a soldier and the son of a great soldier. He believed in his country. George Washington was his hero. He regarded the institution of slavery as the curse of the South.

Yet deep in the stream of his life was a love for Virginia that defied words or logic. It was a current stronger than all else. And in the spring of 1861, staring into the face of a terrible dilemma, he put his thoughts in letters:

"As far as I can judge by the papers, we are between a state of anarchy and civil war. May God avert both of these evils from us!

"As an American citizen, I take great pride in my country, her prosperity and her institutions, and would defend any State if her rights were invaded. But I can anticipate no greater calamity for the country than a dissolution of the Union. It would be an accumulation of all the evils we complain of, and I am willing to sacrifice everything but honor for its preservation."

Then he penned a doubt that weighed heavily on his mind: "Still, a Union that can be maintained only by swords and bayonets, and in which strife and civil war take the place of brotherly love and kindness, has no charm for me. If the Union is dissolved and the Government disrupted, I shall return to my native State and share the miseries of my people; and save in defense, will draw my sword on none."

On April 17, the tyrant hand of fate touched his shoulders. That day, General Scott sent a message to Arlington, enclosing a note from a close friend of Lincoln's, inviting the Virginia colonel to meet him in the famous Blair House across the street from the White House.

Lee was privately regarded by the President as first choice for leadership of the Federal Army. He looked the part of nobility: he had a keen, searching mind, an intuitive sense that seemed almost to read other men's minds: troops followed him unfalteringly. When Lee received the letters, he knew they were the summons to leadership.

On the morning of April 18, he stood alone on the portico of Arlington House. This moment contained all he loved — the beauty of spring, the serenity of a happy home, a soul at peace with his God. But he was a soldier, and a good soldier must steel his mind for any fate.

It was in this mood that he met the President's friend at Blair House, and was offered command of the Federal Army being organized to defend Washington. Lee's clear eyes were sober, his voice was gentle when he refused. He said with strong feeling that he opposed secession, but that he could not lead an invasion of the South.

Next morning, on a business errand in Alexandria, Lee read the news he dreaded. Virginia had seceded! He turned homeward, his heart burdened with apprehension. By the time he reached Arlington House, it was filled with anxious neighbors and friends. Some cursed the Union, others shook their heads with concern.

Lee patiently listened to all. Through the day, the crowds and the clamor disturbed the usual peace of Arlington.

Late in the day, Lee escaped into the yard to be alone. He stared long at the city of Washington, below and beyond the Potomac. The lights were bright in the State-War-Navy Building, next to the White House on Pennsylvania Avenue. Even at that moment, Lee knew, his superiors were planning to guard Washington by an attack on Virginia. That would be his choice, too, if he were shaping strategy.

Lee's boots crunched on the stone path as he turned into the rose garden full of buds, down the carriage driveway and past the ivy-covered tomb of Mary Randolph. The fragrance of spring was all about him.

When Lee finally returned to the house, he was as dignified as ever, but gave no hint of his decision. Slowly he walked up the wooden stairs in the rear of Arlington House, and soon his measured footsteps were heard by his friends waiting below.

Lee was in his bedroom, so simple a room as to be austere — a fireplace, a four-poster bed, chests of drawers, a mirror with an eagle carved in the frame.

Some time after midnight, the troubled pacing stopped. Lee knelt in prayer, then arose and wrote two letters — one to the Secretary of War resigning his commission, the other to General Scott advising him:

"I would have presented it (my resignation) at once, but for the struggle it cost me to separate myself from a service to which I have devoted all the best years of my life and all the ability I possessed . . .

Save in defense of my native State, I never again desire to draw my sword."

His anxious wife met Lee at the foot of the stairway. He spoke to her in the composed tone of one who has thrown off a great burden: "Well, Mary, the question is settled." A few days later, he accepted command of Virginia's troops.

Often in the next four years the peace of Arlington House must have called to him, for Lee loved life and hated destruction. After Gettysburg, he wrote in passionate despair: "The loss of our gallant officers and men causes me to weep tears of blood and to wish that I never could hear the sound of a gun again."

And in 1865, when surrender was forced upon him by the needless slaughter of his troops, his General Order of April 10 declared: ". . . But feeling that valor and devotion could accomplish nothing that could compensate for the loss that would have accompanied the continuance of the contest, I determined to avoid the useless sacrifice of those whose past services have endeared them to their country."

Many of his officers wanted to continue the struggle underground and organize guerilla bands. But Lee answered sternly: "No, that will not do! We have fought this fight as long as, and as well as, we know how. We have been defeated. For us, as a Christian people, there is now but one course to pursue. These men must go home and plant a crop, and we must proceed to build up our country on a new basis."

In defeat, Lee revealed a greatness even more profound. He was Lee, the healer of wounds of the spirit; Lee, the loyal American who preached by word and deed: "Love your enemies, bless them that curse you, do good to them that hate you, and pray for them which despitefully use you."

When, after the war, a Southern woman bitterly cried out against the North, Lee admonished her to train her sons "to be loyal Americans."

In his own heart there must have been pain, for Arlington House was taken as a prize of war, its rooms and gardens plundered. And yet today there is union beyond the power of anyone to cleave it, and Arlington, restored as the home of Lee, is in a sense a memorial to that cause.

The silence of these peaceful acres is broken only by the sound of shots fired into the air and the brave call of "Taps," floating up from Arlington Cemetery. On these days, memory recalls the sad, thoughtful Lee as he stood on the heights at Fredericksburg, reviewing the bright pageantry of battle. There before him advanced the Union lines of blue-clad troops, the sun shining on their muskets, regimental flags flying boldly, the bands playing brassy, stirring music. It was then that Lee said: "It is well that war is so terrible, or we should grow too fond of it."

The Capitol

8. Dome of Liberty

NO sight in all the beauty of Washington so stirs the hearts of men as the dome of the Capitol rising from the night. There, standing proudly alone on the crest of the hill, glowing under floodlights like a jewel on the black velvet cape of night, she is Freedom.

A Senator-elect, coming to Washington after nightfall, saw the dome above the gray and broken skyline as he crossed the Memorial Bridge. "I felt strangely humble, as if I were in the presence of a higher spirit," he wrote a friend. "All the pride and arrogance of what I, as a Senator, would do melted away. I knew then that men alone cannot guide a nation. A greater power must lead them."

Others recall the buried words of a Roman poet who saw in a dream "the great white dome, the peoples' shrine." Yes, this is a peoples' shrine. The priceless tile floors, the majestic sweeping stairways, are worn with the steady tread of the people . . . great and little, rich and poor, wise and foolish. Laughing barefoot Negro children, boys in the khaki of enlisted men, and the stern white hair of age stand side by side before the statues and portraits. They mingle in the halls with Senators, Representatives, Cabinet members.

A Capitol historian, George Hazelton, Jr., who saw this democracy of time and caste, was moved to write: "The great pile is national, American, human. On its walls are written the nation's history. Its corridors resound to the footsteps of her living heroes and sages; its every stone echoes the departed voices of her greatest dead."

The Capitol is much more than a shrine. It is a faithful observer of the growing strength of the United States. It is a cathedral in the great, glowing room under the dome. And it is a stage for a constant drama as thundering as the Old Testament.

The Capitol, as the observer, has seen Washington grow from a capital of rude simplicity and hope, through defeat and trial, to a power undreamed of even by a Caesar.

In the beginning, when it was known as "Congress House," the Capitol stood on an isolated hill where the Powhatan Indians once lit their tribal fires. Shanties, ditches and rutted roads were in the forest below. Pennsylvania Avenue was a bog covered with alder bushes and scrub oak. A Secretary of the Treasury wrote disdainfully, "There are few houses in one place, and most of them are miserable huts."

Late in the summer of 1814, invading British troops burned the Capitol to avenge the American raid on Toronto and the burning of Parliament. A witness to this savagery wrote: "In the Hall of Representatives the devastation was dreadful. There was no 'want of materials for conflagration. All the stages and seats of the galleries were of timber and pine. The British made a great pile in the center of the furniture and set fire to a quantity of rocket stuff in the middle. The whole was soon ablaze and so intense was the flame that the glass of lights was melted. The exterior of the columns scaled off and not a vestige of sculpture or fluting remained."

At the cornerstone laying for the reconstruction, Daniel Webster bravely told the world: "Be it known on this day, the Union of the United States stands firm; that their Constitution still exists unimpaired and with all its original usefulness and glory, growing every day stronger and stronger."

Twenty years later, the Union was divided. The faint roar of civil war could be heard from the Capitol terrace, and the building itself was in part a barracks. As time moved patiently on, Mark Twain stood in the dome and looked west on "a quiet pastoral locality . . . cowsheds about its [the Washington Monument] base and contented sheep nibbling pebbles in the holy calm of its protecting shadow."

Today, the occasional visitor who toils up the tortuous winding 365 steps to the dome sees only majesty and might.

The dome is, in a sense, a lighthouse for the free world. Years ago, huge lanterns shone out from the dome when Congress was in night session. They were placed in the narrow columned space between the dome and the huge, bronze statue, the Goddess of Freedom, on top. In modern times, except for the World War II blackout, floodlights illumine the dome in the hours of darkness.

On stormy nights when the Fates are angry, lightning — jagged and awful — seems to spring from the Goddess' plumed head-dress and shield. Of this nineteen-foot work of art, the sculptor wrote: "She represents 'armed Liberty.' She rests upon the shield of our country, the triumph of which is apparent by the wreath in the same hand which grasps the shield; in her right hand she holds the sheathed sword to show the fight is over for the present, but ready for use whenever required. The stars upon her brow indicate her heavenly origin; her position upon the globe represents her protection of the American world — the justice of whose cause is apparent in the emblems supporting it."

The goddess's headdress is Americana, a helmet topped by an eagle's head and feathers. The sculptor's original plan was a simple cap, the age-old symbol of freedom. But Secretary of War Jefferson Davis, later president of the Confederacy, objected violently. The cap was the Roman badge of emancipation; when a slave was freed he was given a cap. Davis wanted no such antislavery propaganda atop the Capitol, so the sculptor was forced to search for a symbol as native to America as corn and tobacco.

Within the dome is a cathedral, a place of worship for the thousands of tourists who pass through the bronze doors daily. Even on those gloomy dark days which seem to brew storms, in the chambers a mellow light touches the rotunda. It gives life to the indescribably sad eyes of Lincoln, and lights up the fiercely independent face of Jackson. It gives a softly religious glow to the fresco in the eye of the dome, showing the deification of Washington.

The past, the present and the future gather in this cathedral. The heroic past is enshrined in paint, marble and bronze. The leaders of today, their foreheads creased with the cares of the moment, stride through the rotunda with no time for yesterday. And somewhere in the crowd of eager school kids, there is a future Senator, perhaps a President.

America's past begins with the magnificent bronze doors on the east. The path of Christopher Columbus is boldly carved out of cold metal. In the main panel above the transom, Columbus, a finely carved miniature figure, finds the New World. He stands triumphantly on a mound of shore. Below him, a sailor prays, and natives crouch behind a tree in fright.

Behind Columbus, the conquerors, the messengers of civilization — soldiers in coats of mail — stare curiously at the unfamiliar scene. Other panels trace Columbus's life from the day the Council of Salamanca, wise men who saw heresy in new thoughts, sneered at his claim the world was round, to his humble death.

The dramatic canvases that splash the great walls of the rotunda are of the hard birth of a new nation — "Signing of the Declaration

of Independence," "Surrender of General Burgoyne," "Baptism of
Pocahontas," "Surrender of Lord Cornwallis" . . . The figures in this
latter portrait faithfully follow an eye-witness account: "At about
12 o'clock the combined army (American and French) was drawn
up into two lines more than a mile in length, the Americans on the
outside of the road, the French to their left. Washington, mounted
on a noble steed and attended by his staff, was in front of the former.

"The French troops in complete uniform and well-equipped
made a brilliant appearance, and had marched to the ground with
a band of music playing. The American troops, but part in uniform,
and all in garments much the worse for wear, yet had a spirited
soldier-like air. At about 2 o'clock the (British) garrison sallied
forth and passed through with shouldered arms, slow and solemn
steps, colors cased and drums beating a British march. They were
all well-clad, having been furnished with new suits prior to their
capitulation. In passing through the line formed by the allied army,
their march was careless and irregular, and their aspect sullen. The
order to ground arms was given by their platoon officers with a tone
of deep chagrin, and many of the soldiers threw down their arms
with a violence sufficient to break them."

The other moments of American history on canvas in the rotunda
are George Washington resigning his commission as commander in
chief of the Revolutionary Army, the landing of the Pilgrims, Columbus reaching America, and De Soto's discovery of the Mississippi.

Against the west wall of the rotunda is a face as memorable
as death. The sadness haunts visitors years later. This is Gutzon
Borglum's head of Lincoln, rising from a block of marble. Here is
the Lincoln who suffered with every mother of a fallen soldier, who
looked with each prisoner through the bars at freedom beyond.

From above, the fresco in the eye of the dome is the loving labor
of a genius, Constantino Brumidi, the "Michaelangelo" of the
Capitol. He was a captain of Papal Guards, thrown into prison and
exiled because his ideas of freedom clashed with authority. He
came to America as a pilgrim to a shrine, and, when he was naturalized, proudly signed his paintings, "Citizen of the U.S."

He once said: "I have no longer any desire for fame or fortune. My one ambition and my daily prayer is that I may live long enough to make beautiful the Capitol of the one country in which there is liberty."

This prayer was painted on wet plaster, loving and with a talent few men can equal. Of this fresco, one critic wrote: "Clouds of gold, azure and rose seem hanging there, spanned by a rainbow and, floating among them, forms of exquisite beauty. Grand mythological figures, symbolizing Force and Progress, appear there, too — titanic, majestic — almost appalling with their great significance."

The central figure is George Washington, the savior, a robe over his knees, a sword in his left hand, surrounded by the Goddesses of Victory and Liberty and thirteen angels. Below him, Freedom, a Joan of Arc figure with a red, white and blue shield, strikes down the villains of Tyranny, Kingly Power, Anger, Vengeance and Discord.

In other allegories in this fresco, Young America shows Ceres, Goddess of the Harvest, how his two plunging horses can pull the American reaper. The giant Vulcan, symbol of our mechanical progress, stands with his right foot on a cannon while his workmen labor at forges. The winged Mercury, God of Commerce, holds a bag of gold for Robert Morris, financier of the Revolution. The great bearded Neptune rises from the sea on two mighty steeds, while the most beautiful of all the goddesses, Aphrodite, holds the Atlantic cable.

Such early American intellects as Benjamin Franklin, Robert Fulton and Samuel F. B. Morse are in attention about Minerva, Goddess of Wisdom. All these are in colors that glow like the sunlight streaming through the windows of the dome.

Throughout the Capitol there is the touch of Brumidi's affection and genius — the frieze encircling the rotunda, the bronze stairs of angels and flowers to the House Chamber, the wonder and rich flourishes of the President's room off the Senate Chamber. (This is a museum which an occasional stray visitor discovers and faces with awe. It is like a room from a very old edition of fairy tales, full of rich colors, plump cherubs, a giant golden mirror which might, if you wish hard enough, have magic powers, and remarkably lifelike portraits of Washington's Cabinet. On the frescoed ceiling the spiritual eyes of the lovely Madonna of Religion follow the visitor in mute appeal.)

In committee rooms tucked away in odd corners of the Capitol, the art and allegory of Brumidi fill walls and ceilings. A sobering look at the past is Washington at Valley Forge. In the bleak snow, Washington wrapped in a cape looks on a group of his soldiers, one of them barefoot, huddled about a fire. This was to remind Senators studying military affairs in this room of the sacrifice that brought our nation into being.

While Brumidi re-created American history in an ancient art form, the Capitol is filled with examples of pure Americana. One is the six famous "corncob" columns praised by Jefferson. They are in a small ground-floor lobby of the Senate wing. At the top of the columns are ears of corn. There are small holes in the columns, and the guards swear they must have been made by bullets in some long-past, unrecorded duel within the Capitol.

Not many steps distant, in the low-ceilinged room where the guide remarks impressively, "There are nine million pounds over your head," is another example of distinctly American art. It is the valiant, strong, believing heads of three women rising from a block of stone. There are Lucretia Mott, Susan B. Anthony, and Elizabeth Cady Stanton, pioneers in the fight for women's suffrage.

Over the steps to the House Gallery is a stirring mammoth painting of a wagon train crossing the Rockies. The pioneers stand weary but elated, looking at the beauty and columns of smoke beyond in the promised land. And, outside, the design over the eastern steps to the Capitol was suggested by President John Quincy Adams. One afternoon during a storm, Adams took shelter under an arch and there found the artist and gave his ideas.

For those who like their drama fresh, strong, sometimes crude, there is no stage in America like the Capitol. Where else could a valiant war hero plead for more arms for his men, and sink his head aching from sickness and weariness on a table? Where else could a strange, slack-mouthed man peer through the smoky haze of a crowded room, point his finger at a disdainful, aloof high government official and call him a traitor who led a double life? Where else could a scientist describe with fear his own creation, the atomic bomb?

These are scenes from Congressional Committee hearings. Almost every day, in some cranny of the Capitol, these hearings unfold before fascinated audiences of Congressmen, reporters and lobbyists.

After the struggles of the day, peace comes at dusk to the Capitol. On a June night, the people of Washington, young and old, of every color and creed, sit undisturbed on the lawn while the Navy Band plays light, joyful music.

From the west terrace is a view no artist could draw. Overhead the American flag flutters in the still blue sky. On either side of the

Photograph from the Library of Congress

terrace, the air is fragrant with white magnolia. Ivy creeps up the stone railings. Over the broad lawn squirrels scamper gaily, while song sparrows sing from the giant old trees. Straight ahead, the Washington Monument, a sword of stone, rises against a brilliant sky — streaks of red, tipped with gold and bands of orange, shoot from the Virginia hills as from some distant, awful fire. Above, gray veils of clouds drift aimlessly.

There, at last, is a haven where the confused, overladen Congressman can find a peace that all men need.

ETERNAL VIGILANCE
IS THE PRICE OF LIBERTY

Photograph from the Library of Congress

The National Archives Building

9. Altar of Democracy

O N clear mornings in Washington, a sword of sunlight awakens a sacred American shrine. As early traffic clatters cheerfully along Constitution Avenue, the sword strikes two massive bronze doors guarding the National Archives. The doors glow with a strange radiance, like the sun pouring from under an edge of cloud.

All day long this radiance beckons pilgrims to worship at an altar of freedom. They come in crowded buses with the dust of Kansas on them, in cars with licenses as far away as Alaska; they come dressed in the severe black garb of the Amish farmers of Pennsylvania, in the flowing *saris* of the Far East, and in the high-heeled boots of the Western plains.

They climb a noble tier of steps past a sculptured Guardian with a legend, ETERNAL VIGILANCE IS THE PRICE OF LIBERTY, and through stately columns to a hall of simple majesty. A few of the pilgrims are pushed in wheelchairs before the altar, and others are tenderly carried in their mothers' arms, that they may early sense their nation's heritage.

They come to see with their own eyes the fading handwriting of the Declaration of Independence, the aged parchment of the original Constitution, and the living freedom of the Bill of Rights. These and other treasured documents of a people's liberty are here for all to view in the Archives, a classic temple on Constitution Avenue.

This is the final resting place of the three great charters of American freedom. The parchments came to life in the heroic birth of America. When British raiders marched on Washington in 1814, the documents were stuffed in crude linen bags and hidden in a grist mill across the Potomac. The Declaration of Independence is faded by sunlight's long stare from hanging for a generation in the Patent Office Building. Later, the parchments were exhibited in the Library of Congress for nearly three decades, except when they were taken during World War II to the bullion depository deep underground at Fort Knox, Kentucky. Then, in 1952, they came to this resting place in the Archives. The documents are guarded with a loving vigilance so that no catastrophe short of God's vengeance may destroy them. The bronze doors are the largest in the world. The minds of science devised a steel and concrete crypt, bomb-proof, shock-proof and fireproof, in which the documents are tenderly lowered at night and in times of peril, as well as a sealed case filled with the ageless papers and a preserving gas. Ingenious filters further shield the sacred words from the withering glare of ultraviolet rays. But no genius has found a way to preserve the freedom from man's own neglect.

Long before the stone temples of government on Constitution Avenue are astir with the clamor of today, the pilgrims are on the Archives' steps waiting for the mammoth doors to slide open on their steel tracks at nine o'clock. On a recent morning, the first group included a ten-year-old boy with an appealing eagerness and a casual part in his sandy hair. His father looked willing, but sleepy.

A spare, white-haired New Englander with steel-rimmed glasses and his gentle-faced wife glanced at the child with kindly attention. A man of dark complexion and yellow sports shirt turned his face lazily to the sun. A pretty girl with a sparkling new wedding ring teased her lanky young man with gay glances.

They watched the huge doors glide noiselessly open and heard a voice from the cool interior say pleasantly, "You can come in now, folks."

They entered a domed, semicircular chamber. An altar at the rear was guarded by two sets of marble pillars — the outer pair a glowing rose color with eagles perched atop them high above the floor; the inner a rich and dark green. Gold letters on a black marble

shield proclaimed: THE DECLARATION OF INDEPENDENCE, THE CON-
STITUTION OF THE UNITED STATES OF AMERICA AND THE BILL OF RIGHTS.
The boy's eyes were wide with wonder.

The small group waited, dazzled and undetermined, in the lobby.
The guard prompted them, "You can go right on in." Humbly they
moved across the stone floor and up the few steps into the shrine
room. They passed through a bronze gate, now flung back to admit
the pilgrims, and noticed on either side the massed flags of the
States. They stared in wonder at the great murals on the curving
walls.

To the left, a tall, noble and red-haired Thomas Jefferson presented the Declaration of Independence to the presiding officer of
the Continental Congress. Here and there in the assembly were
familiar figures from history books . . . Benjamin Franklin, John
Hancock, Samuel Adams. . . . In the mural to the right, a figure of
rare dignity and composure, George Washington, stood in the center
accepting the Constitution from James Madison under the shade of
an ancient tree.

The altar is slightly elevated, with an American flag on each side.
The first and last pages of the Constitution, and the Bill of Rights,
are in a long low case with bronze frame. The Declaration is in a
separate case against the wall. A small bench of marble rests before
the altar.

A guard in uniform nodded to the visitors. He was silver-haired
and comfortably stout, and spoke in a friendly drawl:

"This is the Altar of Freedom. Lots of people ask us what that
little bench is there. That's a kneeling stool, just like you have in
church. The Constitution is the face of the altar; and the Declaration is placed above it, like the Bible opened for the sermon. They're
sealed in helium gas under glass."

The boy pressed closer to see the famous documents. His father
put a hand on his shoulder and said with quiet conviction: "These
papers are what made us great."

"What do you mean, Dad?"

His father pointed to the faded writing on the parchment above

National Archives Photograph

them. "You can't see the words clearly, son," he explained, "but when Washington and Jefferson and the other great men in these paintings started America, they wrote this Declaration. And they told us about a new kind of religion — democracy — in these words: '. . . that all men are created equal, that they are endowed by their Creator with certain unalienable Rights, that among these are Life, Liberty and the pursuit of Happiness.'"

The guard and the man in the sports shirt were listening quietly. So were the honeymooners who had come behind them. The pretty girl's eyes were big and serious.

"This means, son, that everyone is alike, rich or poor, big or little, and that God has given us all the right to live and be free and happy. That's what democracy means."

The boy nodded. His father motioned to the Constitution. "They wrote this democracy into the Constitution in laws. Later, they added to the Constitution a Bill of Rights in ten amendments to

National Archives Photograph

make sure all the freedoms were put down in law. The Bill of Rights says you can speak freely, write freely in your newspapers, worship as you choose, meet freely, that you cannot be seized and put in jail because a dictator has a grudge against you, that police cannot search your house just for the heck of it, and that you have a fair trial."

"Why do we have all this, Dad?" the boy asked.

"Under our kind of government, people are happier; they work harder, and they fight to defend it. You never know how good it is until you lose it."

The man in the sports shirt said gruffly: "You can say that again, Mister! I was in one of those Red prisoner-of-war camps in Korea."

This serious talk was fine for adults, but the boy had questions. "Is that really George Washington's writing?" he asked, pointing to the Constitution's last page. There was the firm, clear signature, *G. Washington, President and Deputy from Virginia.* The guard spoke. "Sure is, son. That tiny writing there is James Madison. And over there, those fancy letters are Ben Franklin. On the Declaration of Independence, John Hancock wrote real large and heavy. You can still see it. He said he didn't want the King of England to put on specs to see his name."

The spare New Englander and his wife had been moving thoughtfully among the cases below the murals. There, in careful script, were the reasons that first brought the bitter Colonists together under the Articles of Association in the bright autumn of 1774: "To obtain redress of these grievances which threaten destruction to the lives, liberty and property . . . we firmly agree and associate under the sacred ties of virtue, honour and love of our country . . ."

And, down the line, was another blueprint for freedom, the Ordinance of 1787 for governing the Northwest Territory, guaranteeing such basic rights as freedom of worship, trial by jury, the writ of *habeas corpus,* and abolishing slavery in this vast area.

The couple went on to the last document. This was Washington's inaugural address when he left the peace of Mount Vernon and spoke soberly of "the magnitude and the difficulty of the trust to which the voice of my country called me."

At last, the two elderly people were drawn to the altar. The old man told her in his crisp New England voice: "Mother, you have to stand a while and let it sink in."

They were silent until she came to the signatures below the Constitution. Then she said wistfully: "Oh, John, it's too bad we don't have such great men today!"

He answered gently but with conviction: "We became a nation and we grew strong because we had faith in ourselves and our cause. That's all we need today."

Then they stood motionless, these two Americans, silently praying before their nation's Altar of Freedom and Democracy.

Entrance Hall of Blair House

10. Shadows of the Great

A KINDLY old grandfather clock is an ally of history. This discreet gentleman, ticking patiently in a quiet hallway, has overheard a thousand secrets from the lips of Presidents, Prime Ministers and Kings. It has listened to the chilling sound of assassins' bullets, and may yet chime the hours for statesmen guiding the world to peace.

It stands at the end of a narrow entrance hall, facing all who pull the great brass knocker on the Georgian mansion at 1651 Pennsylvania Avenue, cater-cornered from the White House. This is Blair House, where Presidents have been made, wars planned, and the United Nations charted.

Throughout the mansion there is a warmth that can be sensed. A mellow glow fills every room. Each piece of furniture, like the philosophic old Simon Willard clock in the hall, belongs there. Outside is the hubbub and pressure of Washington; within is a tranquillity almost unknown in modern life.

The visitor enters on a white marble floor, edged in black. He stands beneath a crystal chandelier while he leaves his calling card on a marble stand and views himself in a mirror, framed in gold leaf and topped by a figure of a proudly aloof bird, the heron. Nearby is the bust of a man with a strong face, Francis Preston Blair, one of America's early king makers.

Ever since Blair House was built in 1824, on a dusty lane known then as President's Square, it has been a key to history. For more than a century it was a private home; today, it is the mansion where visiting heads of state are quartered by the United States Government.

Into this house have come the dancing eyes of Dolly Madison, the rugged purpose of Andrew Jackson, the melancholy of Abraham Lincoln, the smile of William Howard Taft, the moving voice of Franklin D. Roosevelt, the aggressiveness of Harry Truman, and even the sour suspicions of a Soviet leader, V. M. Molotov.

Blair House is an example of sturdy, beautifully simple American architecture, brought into being by shipwrights who once created the fast clipper ships. Their art — an affection and pride in each piece of work — is seen in the old-fashioned heavy doors with large brass key holes and in the delicately carved moldings.

On the outside, Blair House has an unbroken front, large windows and green shutters against a buff-colored wall. A rose bush winds up alongside the wrought-iron railing to the door. Near the entrance a small plaque says: *In honor of Leslie Coffett, White House guard who gave his life in defense of the President of the United States here at Blair House, Nov. 1, 1950.*

The Washington of 1824, when hammers sounded across the square, was a village boldly shaping the world for tomorrow. The Monroe Doctrine had just freed America from Europe's jealous hands. Henry Clay stared into the future and foretold: "This government is to last, I trust, forever; we may at least hope it will endure until the wave of population, cultivation and intelligence shall have washed over the Rocky Mountains."

Debate that later flamed into civil war was raging over the Missouri Compromise. (Francis Blair pleaded with John C. Breckinridge not to seek repeal of the Compromise, and said prophetically: "John, if you do it, you will live to see this country deluged in blood from one end to the other.") The giants of Congress, Daniel Webster of New Hampshire and John C. Calhoun, fiery South Carolinian, met often at Blair House.

Under the first owner, Dr. Joseph Lovell, the house was a social center. Under the second, Francis Blair, the mansion became a

cloakroom of history early in the Andrew Jackson administration. Here the "kitchen cabinet" gathered. Here were planned the speeches delivered in Congress, and the strategy of the political wars. Talks that led to forming the Republican Party and nominating Lincoln took place beneath the glass chandeliers.

A last-minute effort was made in Blair House in 1861 to keep the United States from tearing apart. Old General Blair pleaded with both sides for moderation, and begged his friends, Jefferson Davis and Robert E. Lee, to stay with the United States.

General Scott invited Lee to Blair House and, with Lincoln's approval, offered him command of the Union Armies. Lee refused, but other Dixie friends, such as General William Tecumseh Sherman and Admiral David Farragut, helped lead the North to victory.

Often during the Civil War, the tall gaunt Lincoln strode across the dusty lane in his black suit and stove-pipe hat, and slipped into

Blair House from the garden in rear. In this sanctuary he escaped the pressures of his office, the tragedy of a nation divided, and a nagging wife.

Yet, as close as Blair House has been to the tides of the past, it is even nearer to the crashing history of modern times. The World War II alliance with Russia, the two-ocean strategy against the Axis, the organization of the United Nations, all were plannd in part here. The Marshall Plan was born at a dinner by candlelight, and the lonely decisions to fight Communism in Korea and to make the hydrogen bomb were made over a huge family Bible upstairs.

In a small office off the hallway, a handsome leather guest book holds the key to a strange story. There, under May 29–June 3, 1942, is an almost illegible scrawl — V. M. Molotov. None of the newspaper files of that date mention this visitor from the Soviet Union. The truth is Molotov was secretly visiting Washington to forge an alliance at the moment that Hitler was planning the attack on Stalingrad. The round-faced Russian Foreign Commissar was known simply among those in on the secret as "Mr. Brown."

Molotov's behavior then — and during a later visit in 1945 — is a clue to the mystery of Soviet Russia. Suspicion filled the friendly mansion when the Russians moved in. Cleaning maids were followed everywhere by taciturn secret police. The high canopied beds were systematically unmade after the maids left, and the covers pulled up so one could see beneath the bed.

The change in Russia's fortunes from 1942 to 1945 is dramatically shown in Molotov's second entry in the guest book. Gone is the nervous uncertainty of his signature; it is assured, even arrogant.

The Blair House parlors are museums of good living in a gracious, unhurried age — an Adam chair, Queen Anne secretary, Chinese Chippendale settee, Herez oriental rugs, a Broadwood piano (one of the first in this country), a gray marble fireplace, Ming lamps — all priceless antiques. The half-moon tables in the rear drawing room came from Europe on the ship that brought Lafayette. The deep Chippendale chairs are covered with elaborate needlepoint more than a century old.

Yet none look out of place. They belong there as surely as the carved moldings touching the floor and ceilings. They still invite the guest to enjoy them.

When the Government took possession of Blair House, professional decorators determined to modernize it. It was too old-fashioned, they said, for a gleaming world of chrome and glass. The hostess protested with the fury of a mother protecting her young. The battle swayed back and forth until one Sunday, the French doors to the garden pushed open and President Franklin Roosevelt entered in his wheelchair. Carefully and affectionately he studied every room and asked questions: Then he announced:

"No one has a right to change Blair House. It belongs to all the American people, and is part of their history."

What unknown tales of this history the Waterford chandelier in the dining room could tell! Everything in the room encourages quiet confidences — Lowestoft china made in China and sent to England to be glazed in blue and gold, Battersea candlesticks of porcelain over metal, a sturdy cherry sideboard and table, hanging shelves of Chinese Chippendale, a Paul Revere tankard, a bracket candlestick holder whose glass reflector has a peacock painted on it.

Here, in this room, plans for organizing the United Nations were born. In early January, 1946, a preliminary group from China, France, Iraq, Uruguay, Yugoslavia, Britain and Russia, with Trygve Lie, first Secretary-General, lived here for several days. And at dinner they came together to exchange ideas.

The dining room in the Blair-Lee House (there is no wall between the houses) was a stage for more recent history. During the three and a half years that President Truman lived here while the White House was being remade, the Cabinet had lunch with him every Friday. On one occasion, General George C. Marshall, then Secretary of State, spoke earnestly of friendly nations:

"Their farms and factories were destroyed by war. The Communists are feeding on their misery and gaining recruits. We must help our friends help themselves. We can help them rebuild their economies by dollars, food and fuel."

Photograph from the Department of State

Truman said excitedly, "That's a great idea, General! And we'll call it the Marshall Plan."

Later, Blair House was the scene of one of the most terrible decisions ever laid before a man. The time was June 25, 26 and 27, 1950. The twenty-fifth, a Sunday, was unbearably hot and humid in Washington. The temperature rose to 90°, and thunder rumbled ominously over the city.

Blair House was silent; the Trumans were in Independence, Missouri. In mid-afternoon, bulletins broke into the baseball broadcasts. In the far-off, little-known land of Korea, a Communist army had attacked at dawn.

A grim and troubled President flew back to Washington at 7:20. By 7:45, the government limousines rolled up to Blair House and were greeted by a silent crowd. The President and his advisors gathered in the front drawing room, where the stern face of Webster looks from above the fireplace. The shades were up, and those outside in the gathering twilight saw the tall Secretary of Defense, Louis Johnson, gesturing emphatically, and General Omar Bradley, chairman of the Joint Chiefs of Staff, talking soberly.

The reports from the Far East contained a series of shocks. Communist spies had learned of a major shipment of United States arms to Korea and had struck in advance. The North Koreans were trained and disciplined. They had tanks and modern weapons. Our slim occupation force and the poorly equipped South Koreans could not stop them. This was the pattern of Soviet conquest, like the ill-fated attempt in the Spanish Civil War.

Truman inquired anxiously if this were World War III. Bradley replied cautiously. It might be the first in a series of moves that would draw the world into an atomic war, Korea, then Germany, then Japan, Yugoslavia next, Iran, Greece, and southeast Asia.

"If the Communists are stopped now, will that prevent the spread of war?" the President asked.

The General answered that this was a strong likelihood.

Did General MacArthur have enough forces in Japan to stop the Communist invasion in Korea?

That could be dangerous. Korea might be a diverting move, to pull United States strength away from Japan, and then strike boldly from the Soviet-held Sakhalin Island with indoctrinated Japanese prisoners of war seized in Manchuria in 1945.

With these questions uppermost, the party of thirteen men retired to the dining room for food and more discussion. Three hours later the guests slipped out a side door of Blair House.

Truman walked wearily upstairs to the library, a room which seems almost designed for calm and purposeful thought. A long red carpet has the same design as the woodwork — a pineapple, symbol of hospitality. White bookshelves filled with old volumes surround the room. At one end is an Italian mantel of marble. At the other is the painting of Franklin Roosevelt which he referred to as "my peanut portrait." Old ship's lamps stand on the desk.

Truman drew out a heavy Bible and opened it on the desk. He read steadily for many minutes, making pencil marks on the pages.

This was a habit of his, marking passages that gave him solace or stirred his interest. A casual look today shows on one page these passages noted:

"Three sorts of men my soul hateth, and I am greatly offended at their life; a poor man that is proud, a rich man that is a liar, and an adulterer that doateth. . . . If thou hast gathered nothing in thy youth, how canst thou find anything in thine age. . . . But the love of the Lord passeth all."

The next night, Monday, a calm Truman ordered Johnson to tell MacArthur to send United States planes to assist the South Koreans. The Joint Chiefs of Staff were still reluctant to use ground forces, lest this be a trap. MacArthur was opposed to thinning his ranks in Japan, for the same reason.

On Tuesday night, again at Blair House, Truman announced that American troops, ships and planes would fight for the freedom of Korea. Only the doubts and fears of our Allies would restrain the fury of our counterattacks. The President said simply, we must show the free world that Communism could be stopped before it engulfed the earth. His public statement said, in part:

"The attack upon Korea makes it plain beyond all doubt that Communism has passed beyond the use of subversion to conquer independent nations and will now use armed invasion and war. . . . The United States will continue to uphold the rule of law."

In the Blair House library, with the Bible at his side, Truman made another grave judgment — to manufacture the hydrogen bomb. And the master bedroom across the hall is where Truman was awakened from an afternoon nap by the angry fire of revolvers. He rushed to the window, pulled aside the curtain and saw White House police defending the entrance from two crazed Puerto Rican nationalists. One policeman, one assassin were killed.

Despite such memories, the bedroom is as tranquil as a grove of trees at sunset. From the high bed with a canopy, the awakening statesman can see to his left the long windows that almost touch the floor, before him china figurines of early American folk-singers on the mantel, and priceless Currier and Ives prints on the wall.

On the third floor is a small den where visitors like to browse for an hour. Along two walls are enclosed shelves, holding a collection of early American glass; another wall is a bookshelf with such titles as *Investigation of Naval Contracts, 1860; European Life and Manners;* and the Cottage Bible. The walls are paneled with rare woods shipped from abroad over a century ago and colored with the distinctive Blair dark green.

In this and other rooms of Blair House, history is still to speak. The great brass knocker on the front door will be lifted many times by statesmen yet unknown. If man can be as patient as the grandfather clock in the hall, a lasting peace may yet come to life here.

A conversation by candlelight, a few lines from the family Bible, and hope may be the ingredients. This is the prayer that lives in every quiet room.

The Old Senate Chamber

11. Freedom's Room

A PROUD eagle guards America's room of freedom. He hovers aloof, his claws fiercely gripping a bar, his powerful wings outspread. From this perch above the presiding officer's bench the eagle commands a peaceful, sunlit room in the Capitol.

Old and treasured portraits of American history show the eagle staring boldly on debates that shaped our destiny as surely as a brawny smith twists white hot metal. For this is where John C. Calhoun, trembling with passion, shouted: "Death is not the greatest calamity; there are others still more terrible to the free and the brave!"

Here, too, Daniel Webster spoke a prayerful appeal: "Liberty and Union, now and forever, one and inseparable."

This is the old Senate chamber, today a small and quiet hall with a mellowness only time can bring. It is plain, even humble, compared to the large and gaudy chamber a few steps away where the Senate meets today. Yet a visitor is strangely moved by the past in this silent hall with an arched ceiling and guardian eagle.

It is alive with the long ago. Time has stopped. Even the gold hands on the dignified clock above the bench always point to twelve. Marble busts from the past look out wisely from pillars spaced about the semi-circular chamber. Here and there paint has cracked off the wall.

This is truly America's room of freedom. Within these walls, the Senate found that it alone could halt tyrants and feverish men. Rash

Presidents who would rule like a distant czar were humbled in this room. At other times a House of Representatives, caught in some angry, fleeting passion, was restrained by the Senators. Here, too, where the eagle stands guard, the Senate discovered a great and awful power, the Congressional investigation.

Within our times an aroused Secretary of the Treasury, Andrew Mellon, insisted: "Government by investigation is not government." Aged, wise Senator Carter Glass of Virginia replied: "Conversely, government by suppression is not government."

Today, superstitious old-timers on Capitol Hill say that on moonlit nights ghosts of the past are summoned by the eagle into this room of freedom. Perhaps this is just a dream of foolish people, but what a reward for a spectator brave enough to dare the anger of ghosts! Imagine in the eerie brightness of moonlight Dan Webster in what many call the greatest oration in Congress.

He stands stalwart, facing the eagle, his fist clenched on top of his desk littered with papers and bills. He has a great sloping forehead, heavy black eyebrows, a glint of humor in his deep-set eyes, and a determined jaw. He dresses elegantly in a swallow-tail coat with brass buttons.

Behind Senator Webster, leaning on the railing of the crowded gallery, George Washington looks down from a painting. The gallery is filled with women in long dresses and poke bonnets. The occasion is a crisis of democracy.

Will the union of States hold together with the power of one wave crashing against the beach, or will it pull apart into a thousand little ripples?

"Black Dan," as the Senator is known in the journals, begins with the softness of a practiced orator. Whispering ceases so all can hear. His wife in the gallery leans forward under his peculiar spell. Webster speaks of what the Union has done for all Americans. He pauses and looks full upon the greatest enemy of a strong union, fiery Vice President Calhoun, just under the eagle's wings. Now Webster's voice breaks the stillness like the crack of lightning on a summer night.

"I have not allowed myself, sir, to look behind the Union to see what might lie hidden in the dark recess behind. I have not coolly weighed the chances of preserving liberty when the bonds that shall unite us together shall be broken asunder. I have not accustomed myself to hang over the precipice of disunion, to see whether, with my short sight, I can fathom the depth of the abyss below."

Senator Robert Y. Hayne, who bluntly questioned the authority of the Federal Government, scowls darkly. A deaf, curly-haired Senator cups a hand to his ear. Senator Thomas Hart Benton, his arms folded, stands grimly attentive, leaning against a pillar in the rear of the chamber. Calhoun, dashing and handsome, leans forward with his elbow on the desk.

Webster cries: "While the Union lasts, we have high, exciting, gratifying prospects spread out before us, for us and our children. Beyond that, I seek not to penetrate the veil.

"God grant that in my day at least that curtain may not rise! When my eyes shall be turned to behold for the last time the sun shining in the heavens, may I not see him shining on the broken and dishonored fragments of a once glorious Union: on States dissevered; on a land drenched with civil feuds, or drenched, it may be, in fraternal blood!"

(The visitor may wonder at the mysterious prophecy that weaves in and out of American history. Webster is foreseeing the terrible War Between the States.)

"Let their last feeble and lingering glance rather behold the gorgeous sign of the Republic still full high advanced, not a single star obscured, bearing for its motto no such miserable interrogatory as, What is all this worth?, but everywhere, spread all over in characters of living light, blazing on all its ample folds, as they float over the sea and over the land, and in every wind under the whole heavens, that other sentiment, dear to every true American heart — Liberty and Union, now and forever, one and inseparable!"

It was three years after Webster spoke, on a bleak Friday afternoon in February, 1833, that an impassioned reply was made. Calhoun left the Vice Presidency and ran for the Senate to speak out.

Calhoun led the forces of those afraid of the gathering power of the Federal Government. He and President Andrew Jackson had clashed publicly on this issue. At a political dinner, Jackson proposed a toast, "Our Union, it must be preserved!"

All eyes turned to Calhoun, whose hand shook as he drank the toast, wine spilling over the rim. He offered the next toast, "The Union, next to our liberty, most dear!"

On this February afternoon, the striking Calhoun damned the "extraordinary powers which are proposed to clothe the Executive to the utter prostration of the rights of states, and the rapid progress of despotism in our country."

He challenged: "Has the Government the right to impose burdens on the capital and industry of one portion of the country to benefit another? There is no limitation over the power of the sword, and that over the purse is equally without restraint. It is to South Carolina a question of self-preservation and I proclaim it — should this bill pass, and an attempt made to enforce it, it will be resisted by every hazard, even that of death itself."

Then John Calhoun spoke immortal words, words that have inspired oppressed people the world over. The small Senate chamber, half-covered with the shadow of a winter afternoon, was hushed.

"Death is not the greatest calamity; there are others still more terrible to the free and the brave, and among them may be placed the loss of liberty and honor. There are thousands of her brave sons who if need be are cheerfully prepared to lay down their lives in defense of the State, and the great principles of Constitutional liberty for which she is contending. . . . Disguise it as you may, the controversy is between power and liberty. History furnishes many instances of similar struggles where love of liberty has prevailed against power under every disadvantage."

Next day, Webster again stood on this floor, and the course of America lay in his words: "Senator Calhoun's resolution affirms, in effect, that these twenty-four United States are held together only by a treaty, resting for its fulfillment on the plighted faith of each state — in other words, that our Union is but a League, that it is the good pleasure of every state to decide how long she will choose to remain a member, that any state may resist a law which she herself chooses to say exceeds the power of Congress, that, as a sovereign power, she may redress her own grievances by her own arm."

He added in scorn: "Mr. President, if we are to receive the Constitution as a text and then lay down on the margin the contradictory commentaries by different states, it would speak with as many tongues as the builders of the tower of Babel."

The sequel to this scene has been preserved on canvas and in the yellowed pages of the *Congressional Globe*. It was seventeen years later. Only the eagle looks the same, impervious to time. Webster, tired, dejected, slumped at his desk. Calhoun, stern and gray, stands. The women in the gallery no longer wear poke bonnets and high collared dresses; instead, the long, flowing gown with the low bodice. The Senate is so crowded the presiding officer again and again calls for order. Crowds in the hall outside press, and even voices call out.

Henry Clay, weak with age and a strenuous life, stands facing the eagle, his arms stretched in an appeal. This is the last chance to save the Union, and Clay, "The Great Pacifier," is pleading:

"Never have I risen under feelings of such deep solicitude. I have witnessed many periods of great anxiety, of peril, of danger to my country, but I have never before arisen to address any assembly so appalled, so anxious. And, sir, I hope it will not be out of place to do here what again and again I have done in private chambers — to implore of Him who holds the destinies of nations and individuals in His hands to calm the violence and rage, to still passion to allow reason once more to resume its empire."

The faltering voice gathers strength, and Clay says: "Mr. President, it is passion, passion, party, party, and intemperance that I dread. All now is uproar, confusion, menace to the Union and the happiness and safety of this people. I implore gentlemen, whether from North or South, by all they hold dear — love of liberty, regard for posterity, gratitude to Him, by all the duties they owe mankind — I implore them to pause, solemnly to pause, at the edge of the precipice before the fearful and disastrous leap."

Strangely enough, as though fate willed it, the greatest debates of the Senate are on this theme — unity or disunity. Three generations later, when the Senate had moved to the large, rectangular chamber in the North Wing of the Capitol, the members were driven apart over the League of Nations debate.

The "little group of willful men," as they were bitterly called by a shaken President Woodrow Wilson, held the floor for weeks. The master orator was William E. Borah of Idaho, rough-hewn like a pioneer of the early West, a shaggy mane of hair parted in the center, a positive manner that was well-nigh hypnotic. His voice was deep and resonant, and he spoke with a fascinating meter.

In mid-autumn of 1919, when Washington was beautiful with the glorious colors of dying leaves, Borah arose in the gloomy Senate chamber. It was the present oblong-shaped chamber in the North Wing, the small, mahogany desks arched in a half-circle. The air was stale with old words, for the League had been debated almost continuously for a year. Borah's magic voice demanded:

"What is the meaning of all this? Why are we in the midst of all the affairs of Europe? We have entangled ourselves with all European concerns. Mr. President, we have forfeited and surrendered once and for all the great policy of 'no entangling alliances' upon which the strength of this Republic has been founded for one hundred and fifty years. We are a part of European turmoils and conflicts from the time we enter this League. This treaty is in conflict with the right of our people to govern themselves free from all restraint, legal or moral, of foreign powers."

Borah's words gathered up nagging doubts and threw them at fellow Senators, sitting attentive in their chairs.

"I will not give up my belief that America, not alone for the happiness of her own people, but for the moral guidance and greater contentment of the world, be permitted to live her own life. The distinguishing virtues of a real republic you cannot commingle with the discordant and destructive forces of the Old World, and still preserve them."

These words destroyed the League of Nations. Wilson's reply was an appalling prophecy: "I can predict with absolute certainty that within another generation, there will be another war. What the Germans used in this war were toys compared with what would be used in the next!"

It was a generation later, after a war that leveled the cities of Europe and offered a great human sacrifice, that Borah was finally answered in the Senate. The speaker — and this again shows the mystic irony of our history — was one whose words were hailed by Borah in 1919. He was then a young Grand Rapids editor, Arthur Vandenburg.

This was a different, far wiser Senator Vandenberg who stood handsome by his desk on the right side of the aisle on January 10, 1945. The steel beams erected to protect the Senate against bombs still wove grotesquely across the ceiling. American men were still fighting on alien battlefields.

Vandenberg was not a flaming orator like Calhoun and Borah. But there was a quiet greatness about him. The Vandenberg who stood in the Senate was like an Old Testament figure who had witnessed a revelation that changed his life. He spoke slowly and meaningfully:

"Mr. President, there are critical moments in the life of every nation which call for the straightest, the plainest, the most courageous thinking of which we are capable. We confront such a moment now.

"It is not only desperately important to America — it is important to the world. It is important not only to this generation which lives in blood — it is important to future generations if they shall live in peace. Each of us can only speak according to his lights, and pray for a wisdom that shall lead us to a high, safe ground. It is only in this spirit of anxious humility that I speak today.

"Mr. President, we still have two major wars to win. It must mean one for all and all for one; and it will mean this, unless somewhere in this grand alliance of nations the stupid and sinister policy of ulterior ambitions shall invite the enemy to postpone our own victory through our own rivalries and confusion.

"We also have yet to achieve such a peace as will justify this appalling cost. Otherwise, we shall look back upon a futile shambles and, God save the mark, look forward only to the curses of World War III. . . .

"Since Pearl Harbor, World War II has put the gory science of mass murder into new and sinister perspective. Our oceans have ceased to be moats which automatically protect our ramparts. Flesh and blood now compete unequally with winged steel. War has become an all-consuming juggernaut. If World War III arrives, it will open new laboratories of death too horrible to contemplate."

Vandenberg's voice rose with firmness: "I propose to do everything in my power to keep those laboratories closed for keeps." Then he laid down a new philosophy for America: "I want maximum cooperation, consistent with legitimate self-interest, to make the basic idea of Dumbarton Oaks — international cooperation — succeed. I want a new dignity and a new authority for international law. I think American self-interest requires it."

What were the choices? Vandenberg outlined them like a painter with a few skillful brush marks.

One pattern was the Russian — to surround a nation with buffer states and stare out suspiciously on the world. The other was a world organization which had the power and will to prevent aggression.

Vandenberg asked: "Now which is better in the long view from even a purely selfish Russian standpoint — to forcefully surround herself with a cordon of unwilling controlled states, thus affronting the opinions of mankind, or to win the priceless asset of world confidence by embracing full and wholehearted cooperation in a vital world organization in which all of us shall honorably take part to guarantee that Axis aggression shall never rise again? Well, at that point, Russia — or others like her — can reply: 'Where is any such guarantee until we know what the U. S. will do?'

"We should meet this at once. There is no reason to wait. . . . In honest candor, we have the duty and right to demand that whatever independent actions must be made for military necessity — they shall be temporary and reviewed in the long light of the postwar world and the postwar peace league."

These words, which won the Senate as surely as Borah pulled Senators away from the League a generation before, ended with a hope for all men, for all time.

"We are standing by our guns with epic heroism. I know of no reason why we should not stand by our ideals. I am prepared, by effective international cooperation, to do our full part in charting happier and safer tomorrows. But I am not prepared to guarantee permanently the spoils of an unjust peace. It will not work. We must have united efforts on all fronts, in our councils, and among our peoples."

This ideal still stands before the world, like the dawn of a more perfect tomorrow.

Photograph from the Federal Bureau of Investigation

Headquarters of the FBI

12. Men Against Crime

A GREAT truth is cut into the ageless stone of a government building on Pennsylvania Avenue. The inscription is so high and remote, just under the eaves of the Department of Justice, that few people notice it. But occasionally, someone glances up casually, then stops in wonder. The words are: JUSTICE IN THE LIFE AND CONDUCT OF THE STATE IS POSSIBLE ONLY AS FIRST IT RESIDES IN THE HEARTS AND SOULS OF THE CITIZENS.

A tribute to this inscription is a long line of parked school buses around the corner on quiet Ninth Street. The passengers, hundreds of schoolchildren — the same who noisily clatter up the Washington Monument and race across the Capitol grounds — are inside the Department of Justice building, learning respect for law. They stand deep in the awe that adventure brings the young.

They have entered a daring world where justice always triumphs, where the guilty are found and the innocent freed, where none of the evils that usurp law can live. In the plain, austere offices, men and women are clear-eyed, clean-cut, and reveal a happy devotion to work, like acolytes in an honored religious order.

This is the Federal Bureau of Investigation, a strange and wonderful institution in a twentieth-century world where tyranny is often exercised in the name of police power. Its acts are based not on the suspicious edicts of a despot or the "brooding omnipotence in the sky" of Old Testament codes, but on the enlightened laws of democracy.

The wisdom guiding the FBI is found in the frail parchment of old texts describing the roots of law in America, and in the words of the creator of the modern FBI, J. Edgar Hoover. In a tiny yellowed volume appear guiding phrases:

"These officers [of early America] ought to have especial care for the preservation of public peace; for peace is the very end and foundation of civil society. From the nature and form of our government, the moral character and happiness of the community so much depend upon the due administration of trusts imposed in justices of the peace, it is to be desired that persons of the best information and best qualified be selected and encouraged by the people and government to take upon them this important service."

Hoover took command of the FBI in the mid-Twenties when it was dying of rot, and brightened it into a shining symbol of law and order. Again and again, he was refused extra powers for the FBI and has successfully resisted the cries of those who would have it broadened into a master police agency. His philosophy was disclosed before a Congressional Committee:

"The peace officer must be the servant of the people — protecting their interests and responding to their will. The agency must be an integral part of the community. Otherwise, democratic government would be defiled. . . . The solution of the crime problem is simple: enforce existing laws fairly and impartially, vigorously and relentlessly, and mobilize the full force of education to the facts of crime. . . . We can never have a crime-free America until all who believe in law are united and mobilized against lawlessness. A moral reawakening and a rededication of service to our fellow man can make this a reality."

The young FBI tour leader who greets each group of visiting schoolchildren is the heir of the steady-eyed, nerveless sheriffs whose six-shooters brought law to the old West. This young man, unlike his lusty, two-fisted ancestor, is a college graduate. From his looks, he might have been an Eagle Scout, a first baseman, and president of the student YMCA at a church school. There is nothing in him of the worldly cynic, who parades his disrespect for organized government at the cocktail hour.

Yet he has won the respect of the lawless. One hardened and arrogant killer, the murderer of five policemen, was captured by the FBI and put in a country jail. Squinting through the bars, he gave a younger prisoner this hard-earned advice: "Don't break a Federal law. They'll hunt you down if it takes a thousand years!"

Every week, thousands of young men and women learn in an hour what it took the arrogant criminal half a lifetime to discover. This is the story of what they learn.

The high-school seniors from Loogootee, Indiana, stood in the fifth-floor hall of the FBI and sized up their guide with the shrewdness of youth. The gawky, crew-cut boys decided he could take care of himself in a game or a fight, and that was good enough for them. The girls on the eve of womanhood saw a hundred other things that escape a man: he was good-looking without being sleek, his black hair was neatly combed, he looked you straight in the eye without squirming, his shoes were shined, his fingernails trimmed.

Aware of this test, he opened a door and motioned them in with a smile. The visitors were momentarily confused. The death mask of a notorious criminal, guns of a bandit gang, and a series of minature scenes competed for their attention. The guide's voice captured their interest: "In our country, we want to free the innocent as well as send the guilty to prison. This is the American way." He spoke simply and honestly, as though this was something he believed too deeply to question. "Many innocent men have served a term behind bars for mistaken identity. That's why we are so careful about identification in the FBI."

He pointed to the wall, at two enlarged prison photographs of what appeared to be the same man.

"This proves you can't even trust your own eyes." He turned to the group, picking out the most likely leader, the tall blond youth with a big "L" on his sweater. The tour leader asked him: "Can you tell these two men apart?"

The boy studied every feature intently, then shook his head.

"That's what I would say, too. Scientific measurement with Bertillon instruments would back you up. The length of the ears, the width of the nose, the shape of the head, the size of bones are almost alike. But these men were not even remotely related. Finally, Will and William were distinguished by fingerprints. You can see in these enlarged prints how different their prints were."

The guide moved on to the small scenes, nine stages in the FBI identification of fingerprints. "This is a clearing house. Every day the FBI receives the prints of thousands of suspects and checks them against the master file. Frequently, a man picked up for a minor crime in a small country town is 'big game' — and the prints prove it. Or lost children are reunited with their parents on the basis of this identification."

As he talked, several students moved close to an exhibit. The tour leader joined them.

"This is the story of John Dillinger, the gangster who found out in death that you can't beat the law. There is his death mask, with the scar under his eye where he was shot when he tried to pull a gun on the FBI. This is a pair of dime-store glasses he bought to hide his identity, and a photograph of a girl found in his pocket. . . ."

There, too, was Dillinger's straw hat with the gay blue band, the thirty-five-pound bullet-proof vest, a .45 automatic he converted to a machine gun by a long clip holding thirty shots, a foregrip and a compensator on the end of the barrel. The guide pointed to the hoodlum's fingerprints.

"See the white spots in the center, where Dillinger tried to disfigure his fingerprints by getting a doctor to burn them with acid? It didn't work. There were still 320 points of identity. The doctor was caught, too!"

Reluctantly, the visitors moved away from this exhibit and followed the guide across the room. He observed: "Criminals can be stupid. Here's a man, Roscoe Pitts, who tried to hide his identity and wound up being the most conspicuous fellow in the world."

The youngsters looked up at the photograph of a lanky, barechested figure.

"Pitts was picked up several times and tried to beat the rap by giving aliases. But every time, his fingerprints caught him. So he decided to get rid of them. He had a doctor take the skin off his finger tips and graft skin from his chest. Quite painful, but most successful. The only trouble was, Roscoe Pitts wound up as the only man in the world with completely smooth prints. They were as revealing as if he'd grown a horn in the middle of his forehead."

The Loogootee seniors laughed with the guide.

"And, what's more, there was enough old skin left below the first joint to make positive fingerprint identification."

The visitors lingered briefly at the arsenal of the Barker-Karpis gang, captured in a blazing gun duel. Then they went on to a spy thriller. The guide said cheerfully:

"The FBI used the Nazis' own money to break a spy ring. Harry Sawyer was a naturalized American who visited his mother in Germany, and returned here trained and equipped to build a giant espionage ring. Secret orders — they were stamp-size microphotographs — were hidden in his watch. He had a secret code, and instructions for building a short-wave radio to communicate with Hamburg. Also, he had $1000 to pay off his accomplices.

"That $1000 was turned over to the FBI by Sawyer, because he loved America. He offered to co-operate fully with us. We watched and listened while the spy ring was built. An FBI camera was hiding behind what looked like a mirror, and a microphone was in the room when Frederick Joubert Duquesne, a German master spy for forty years, boasted how he could fool the FBI. He pulled out of his socks blueprints for the new M-1 rifle, and secret plane and torpedo boat plans. Duquesne waved his arms as he bragged. You can see in this picture here — "

The guide pointed to a photograph of a man lolling in a chair, obviously gloating as he spoke. "This was taken in Sawyer's office. See, you can tell the date on the calendar and the time on the clock. That was to make sure the evidence was airtight. Why, Duquesne was so sure the 'window' for the FBI was just a mirror, he even straightened his tie in it. We arrested thirty-two spies, and they got sentences totaling more than three hundred years."

The tall blond boy said, "Gee!"

The guide told them: "Over here is a picture of the Long Island beach where German U-boats landed four saboteurs, while four others landed in Florida. They had $174,588 in American money, enough explosives to cripple our factories and transport, and forged Social Security and draft cards. They were equipped with TNT blocks disguised as lumps of coal, and thermite pen-and-pencil sets that would start fires, and timer devices that would set off explosions two weeks later. On this map, you can see some of the places they meant to blow up — the C. & O. railway tunnels across the Allegheny Mountains, locks in the Ohio River, an aluminum plant in East St. Louis . . ."

"The FBI captured them all within two weeks. Their mission failed."

The wanderers in the maze of law and order followed the guide into the hall and stopped before a glass-paneled office. The visitors pressed their noses against the window. This was the handwriting analysis section with a file of the names, aliases, characteristics, and signatures of fifty-three thousand forgers. Every day, forged checks rain in on the "recognition box" from across the country.

The FBI man explained, "Sixty per cent of the checks that come in here are identified in our files. Our girls have such good memories, they take one look at the check and say, 'Why that looks like the work of Frank Flick.'"

He added philosophically: "Human weaknesses betray even the most cold-blooded criminals. There was a master forger with so many aliases that after one drink, he forgot which one he was using at the moment. He signed the wrong name to a check in a barroom. Now he's in prison!"

Around the corner was a quiet, white-walled laboratory where technicians in gray smocks bent studiously over test tubes and microscopes. The guide spoke proudly: "This is where we free many innocent men. We have samples of all kinds of animal blood in the refrigerator. In the old days, if a suspect had been found near a crime with blood on his clothing, that alone might have convicted him.

Photograph from the Federal Bureau of Investigation

But today, if he protests this is animal blood, we can test it here. We also analyze blood on the undercarriage of cars in hit-run cases."

In another laboratory, where glass instruments bubbled over a gas flame, FBI analysts studied traces of poison — strychnine dropped secretly in whisky, phosphorus in a well-to-do man's medicine, and even, alas, alkali sneaked in grandma's snuff. Down the hall, an orange and white Army parachute was being tested for sabotage. An ugly hole was torn in the nylon. . . . A case over here was filled with neatly catalogued human and animal hairs. . . . Metal compounds were being studied in the spectographic unit. Copper particles are scraped from the knife of a burglary suspect. Are they from the screen cut out of the warehouse basement window?

Another complicated mechanism analyzes the faint smear of paint on a truck's bumper. A Geiger counter checks radioactivity.

Photograph from the Federal Bureau of Investigation

An electronic microscope magnifies twenty thousand times. An ultraviolet light brings out secret writing. . . .

There is a collection of guns and shells from all over the world, even a curious Soviet kind of blunderbuss. The guide explained, "We have one thousand side arms and five hundred shoulder weapons — even a dainty, tiny thing smaller than a cap pistol that actually shoots. These are not just to look at; they are used in solving crimes, to find the kind of weapon used in a killing. The technician there" — he pointed to one bent over a comparison microscope — "is studying the empty shell from a gun that killed a state policeman and comparing it with several others. This is the real secret of the FBI's success. Every fellow here thinks his work is the most important job in the world."

He paused with his group before a door and warned, "Be quiet when we go in here. This is a classroom. FBI agents and police officers from all over the country, and the world too, come here and learn scientific methods of crime detection and new wrinkles in crime."

The Loogootee seniors stood with an awe rarely exhibited in their own classrooms. They looked respectfully at men bent over desk chairs while a lecturer on a stand in front spoke on sabotage.

The guide brought his brood on to another glimpse of the FBI Academy. It was a large room with a center table looking very much like the model towns in electric-train displays. There were miniature lighted factories, a park, apartments, houses, farms, people and animals. The FBI man said:

"We use this diorama to show how to plan a raid; how to hold back traffic, how to move in without tipping the lookouts, how to close off escape routes."

Too soon, the tour was at the finale, the pistol range in the basement. An FBI agent picked up a .38 caliber revolver, made sure the bullets were out, and said seriously: "The first three weeks of practice, we don't even use bullets. We learn and practice the safety rules. . . . Another thing, never point a gun at another unless you want to kill him."

A boy spoke up boldly, "When do you fellows use the guns?"

The agent replied, "Only in self-defense. Then, it's time to shoot."

He sent a silhouette target down the range with the push of a button and turned out the lights. The FBI man stood carefully, steadily, with the pistol in his outstretched arm. There was a sharp flash of lights and a series of deafening roars. Several of the girls screamed. The light back on, two holes were neatly drilled through the skull, three others in a straight line down the stomach.

The blond boy asked seriously: "What does it take to be a good FBI agent?"

The guide replied simply: "On the seal of the FBI are three words, *Fidelity, Bravery, Integrity.* That's what it takes. There is something more, too. I can describe it best by telling about one of our men shot in a gun battle with bank robbers. He lived long enough to identify his killers. When another agent told him to rest, he roused himself for one last word: 'Tell Mr. Hoover I did my best!'"

The Jefferson Memorial

13. Guardian of Democracy

IN a quiet temple in Washington, a soft glow of light touches a
serene face. The face is both strong and tender. Even in the
darkening shades of twilight, it is alive with a wonderful faith. This
is the face of one who has traveled far and hard in search of a
glorious dream, and now, it lies before him.

The commanding figure, tall, erect, unforgettable, is of the American whose brave words remade the world. His words changed it
from a feudal world to one where freedom bursts out in fresh gusts
from continent to continent. This is Thomas Jefferson, whose dream
was democracy. He was President, Secretary of State, Governor,
delegate to the Continental Congress, and author of the Declaration
of Independence. Behind him, cut into marble, are the sacred words
that turn men ever to freedom:

"We hold these truths to be self-evident: That all men are created
equal, that they are endowed by their Creator with certain inalien-
able Rights, among these are Life, Liberty and the pursuit of Happiness, that to secure these Rights Governments are instituted among
men . . ."

The visitor coming here as night gathers has a sense of being alone
on a mountain top with a great and benign force. The long sweep
of steps, the simplicity, the way wind and light fill the round room,
the immortal words cut in stone, and the towering nineteen-foot
statue on a black-granite pedestal create the effect.

The Jefferson Memorial is a pure white temple of breath-taking
beauty. The circular design with a dome, majestic pillars and bold

A. Devaney, Inc., N.Y.

facade is modeled after Jefferson's plan of Monticello, his hill-top home in Virginia. The memorial is on the edge of a peaceful lake, the Tidal Basin, where fishermen linger in the shade of trees and children paddle happily in small boats. The basin is enclosed by a dense thicket of cherry trees where lovers wander unnoticed in the spring.

This site fits ideally into a master plan for Washington. It is as though the Capitol were the handle of a spear and the Washington Monument the end of the shaft; the point formed by the Lincoln Memorial, and the Jefferson Memorial and White House at the sides. The statue of Jefferson looks out through a clearing in the trees to the gardens of the White House and the President's office.

All about the memorial are reminders of the powerful force that he carefully fashioned and set loose in the world. For, as Henry Adams wrote: "Jefferson aspired beyond the ambitions of nationality and embraced in his view the whole future of man."

Every major product of his mind — improved rice seeds, a revolutionary plow to lighten the farmer's burden, the common school system and universal suffrage — were a part of a far-seeing plan. Jefferson wanted to make this land of ours a bright flame of freedom, equality and plenty in a world filled with shadows. He once said:

"A just and solid republican government maintained here will be a standing monument and example for the aim and imitation of the people of other countries; and I join with you in the hope and belief that they will see from our example that a free government is of all others the most energetic; that the enquiry which has been excited among the mass of mankind by our revolution and its consequences will ameliorate the condition of man over a great portion of the globe."

Jefferson's greatest thoughts are etched in four marble panels within the memorial. The great force that pushed him ever onward is cut in letters around the base of the dome: "I have sworn upon the altar of God eternal hostility against every form of tyranny over the minds of man."

What brought this force into being? Look back into Jefferson's boyhood in the Virginia foothills of the Allegheny Mountains. There is the son of a wealthy planter, reading with hungry fascination the soaring lines of Greek and Roman philosophers. They foresaw a day when the ordinary man might break from his cocoon of ignorance and bondage, and they wrote of future model societies. Whatever he read, whatever he saw, Jefferson, as boy and man, asked himself, "What is truth?"

As a college lad in Williamsburg, he saw politics in the raw, for here the Assembly met, and he felt the hot breath of revolution stirring among the people. The Virginia of those days was a colony. Its political policy, religion, economy, and even her future, were dictated by a King and his ministers in another world. The Established Church decreed by the Crown was supported by the colonists' taxes. Learning came from private tutors and libraries, and a few schools of the Established Church. The colonists must ship all their exports to England at a price set in London, and receive back finished goods at an exorbitant rate.

Taxes were written in England. Colonists accused of major crimes were shipped across the sea for trial. This system was supported, in the main, by wealthy merchants and landowners of the Tidewater region. To them, change was peril. But to the rough and independent souls to the west, who crossed the ocean for greater freedom, this was wrong.

Their spokesman was a crude genius, Patrick Henry. His passionate words stirred the young Jefferson as none other. Jefferson stood entranced in the halls and doorways, listening to what he called the "torrents of sublime eloquence of Mr. Henry."

Fascinated, and yet fitting this scene into his background of knowledge, Jefferson, the law student, heard Henry shout to the Virginia Assembly, "Caesar had his Brutus, Charles his Cromwell, and George the Third" — he was interrupted by a cry of "Treason!" from the presiding officer — "may profit by their examples. Sir, if this be treason, make the most of it!"

Jefferson observed, "He appeared to me to speak as Homer wrote. . . . The idol of the country beyond anyone that ever lived."

The young man from Albemarle County was drawn inevitably into politics. At twenty-six, he was sent to the House of Burgesses, the lower chamber of the Virginia Assembly. One of his first acts was characteristic, a bill to emancipate the slaves. This failed, but Jefferson's prophetic words are cut into stone on one of the four panels of the memorial:

"God who gave us life gave us liberty. Can the liberties of a nation be secure when we have removed a conviction that these liberties are the gift of God? Indeed I tremble for my country when I reflect that God is just, that his command cannot sleep forever. Commerce between master and slave is despotism. Nothing is more certainly written in the book of fate than that these people are to be free. . . . "

In the House at this young age, Jefferson bcame a leader who strove to wrest control from older, conservative members. He proposed a day of fast and prayer against British tyranny that was observed throughout the Colony, and he recommended a Continental Congress of all the Colonies to plan united action.

At thirty-one, the red-haired Jefferson wrote the flaming *A Summary View of the Rights of British America,* which drew together the strings of defiance as nothing else. It was a careful indictment of British crimes against freedom, yet filled with such bold (for then) thoughts as:

"Can any reason be assigned why 160,000 electors in the island of Great Britain should give law to 4,000,000 in the States of America, every individual of whom is equal to every individual of them in virtue, in understanding, and in bodily strength?"

Two years later, Jefferson wrote the most far-reaching document of modern times, the Declaration of Independence. It inspired the American Revolution, influenced the French overthrow of monarchy, altered the laws of England, was cried aloud by Latin-American patriots, and even today echoes through Africa and Asia.

Jefferson wrote the Declaration in a rented upstairs room of a German bricklayer in Philadelphia. He was a delegate to the Continental Congress. The magnificent sculptural group above the entrance to the Memorial shows him reading his draft to a committee of the Congress — Franklin, Adams, Sherman and Livingston. It passed in the evening of July 4, 1776, when delegates agreed after three weary days of debate, heat, and swarms of flies from the stables next door.

This was the spark! It was read to cheering throngs and to each brigade of the Continental Army.

To Jefferson, the Revolution was a sacred opportunity to build a workable social order based on the belief that the common man — the English millworker who pushed bravely across the mountains, the sturdy Irish laborer who dug the roads, even the ignorant slave from Africa — was born in the likeness of his Creator. This, Thomas Jefferson set out to construct in the Virginia House of Burgesses, in the Statehouse, and in Washington.

Winston Pote, A. Devaney, Inc., N.Y.

One of the great timbers of this new house was religious freedom. Of this he said: "That duty which we owe our Creator can be directed only by reason and conviction, not by force or violence; and therefore all men are entitled to the free exercise of religion, according to the dictates of conscience." This view he wrote into the famous Virginia Statute of Religious Freedom. From this everlasting document, the second panel of the Memorial quotes:

"Almighty God hath created the mind free. All attempts to influence it by temporal punishments or burthens . . . are a departure from the plan of the holy author of our religion . . . no man shall be compelled to frequent or support any religious worship or ministry or shall otherwise suffer on account of his religious opinions or belief, but all men shall be free to profess and by argument to maintain, their opinions in matters of religion. . . . "

Jefferson added to this the freedoms of the Bill of Rights, which he inspired; universal suffrage, emancipation, release from the economic tyranny of entail (the law guaranteeing one family control of property forever), and free land. Then, in his wisdom, this great philosopher decided man must learn how to rule himself. So public education became another timber of Jefferson democracy. He explained:

"Experience has shewn that even under the best forms, those entrusted with power have, in time and by slow operations, perverted it into tyranny; and it is believed that the most effectual means of preventing this would be to illuminate the minds of the people at large, and more especially to give them knowledge of the facts. Those persons whom Nature hath endowed with genius and virtue should be rendered by liberal education, worthy to receive, able to guard, the secret deposit of the rights and liberties of their fellow citizens, and they should be called to that charge without regard to wealth, birth or other accidental condition or circumstance."

Jefferson was not satisfied with these sturdy foundations for democracy. He rewrote the law code of Virginia, creating a scale of penalty to fit the crimes, and guaranteeing an open trial. He foresaw his country stretching from ocean to ocean, across the great mountain ranges. Jefferson brought men willing to labor for freedom from abroad to break the land with plows, and offered them citizenship in two years. He sent George Rogers Clark into the Northwest to hold it for America. In the Louisiana Purchase, he bought 800,000 square miles of land to the West from Napoleon for $15,000,000.

He also created our monetary system, established the American creed of isolation from the eternal feuds of Europe, and revealed his ever-present fear of tyranny, even in a democratic system, by his proposed Constitution. In the Jefferson plan, there would be no President, but an "Administrator" responsible to a Council elected by Congress.

Jefferson looked far ahead and saw that no system of government could be perfect forever, so he wrote, at the age of seventy-three, what is inscribed in the fourth marble panel of the memorial:

"I am not an advocate for frequent changes in laws and institutions. But laws and institutions must go hand in hand with the progress of the human mind. As that becomes more developed, more enlightened, as new discoveries are made, new truths discovered and manners and opinions change, with the change of circumstances, institutions must advance also to keep pace with the times. We might as well require a man to wear still the coat which fitted him when a boy as civilized society to remain ever under the regimen of their barbarous ancestors."

This prophet and creator of change who stands so sublimely in the Jefferson Memorial was fought savagely at every turn by those who had no faith in the common man. It was as Abraham Lincoln wrote a friend: "The principles of Jefferson are the definitions and axioms of free society. And yet they are denied and evaded with no small show of success. These expressions (of opposition) are identical in object — the supplanting of the principles of free government and restoring those of classification, caste and legitimacy. We must repulse them, or they will subjugate us."

For all the bitterness of his own experience, Jefferson remained to the end a man of hope and vision. Another of the great men of the times, John Adams, wrote despairingly to the seventy-eight-year-old Jefferson, and the latter's reply is an eternal rebuke to all who lose faith:

"Yet I will not believe our labors are lost. I shall not die without a hope that light and liberty are on steady advance. We have seen, indeed, once within the records of history, a complete eclipse of the human mind for centuries. And this, too, by swarms of the same northern barbarians, conquering and taking possession of the civilized world. Should this again be attempted, should the same northern hordes, allured again by the corn, wine and oil of the south, be able to settle their swarms in the countries of their growth, the art of printing alone, and the vast dissemination of books, will maintain the mind where it is, and raise the conquering ruffians to the level of the conquered, instead of degrading these to that of their conquerors. And even should the cloud of barbarism and despotism again obscure the science and liberties of Europe, this country remains to preserve and restore light and liberty to them. In short, the flames kindled on the 4th of July, 1776, have spread over too much of the globe to be extinguishd by the feeble engines of despotism; on the contrary, they will consume these engines and all who work them. . . ."

This is the secret of the faith — alive and wonderful — on the face of the towering figure under the dome!

Photo by Abbie Rowe — Courtesy National Park Service

Ford's Theater

14. "Now He Belongs to the Ages"

ALMOST one hundred years ago, greatness died quietly, like a lingering sigh, in a humble workingman's home. The gaunt body with a face as sad and peaceful as Death itself lay in a bed too short for his length. The simple room was lighted by a gas flare and the gray shadows of dawn. One of the anxious group about the bed, tears in his eyes, whispered: "Now he belongs to the ages!"

Thus Abraham Lincoln, a man of the people, died in a rooming house owned by a Swedish tailor, on the bed of a young soldier from Massachusetts. This simple brick house, and old Ford's Theater across the street, are today a Washington symbol of an undying devotion to a President whose humanity lives long after him. Through the years, millions have come like pilgrims to the theater, now the Lincoln Museum, and to the house where Lincoln died. In the first can be traced step by step, with a scholar's accuracy, the assassination; in the second, the slow ebbing of life.

Ford's Theater stands today, one wall cloaked with ivy, between an appliance store gaudy with advertising and a parking lot. The first floor is a museum rich with mementos of Lincoln; the second and third floors are partly offices, partly a dim and ghostly loft where the spirits of Black Friday, 1865, may well wander to this day.

The background for assassination is there in the exhibit cases — the savage political cartoons of the day which made of Lincoln a grotesque and evil creature, and the small, extravagant handwriting of John Wilkes Booth. There is the mean passion of a madman who exalts his sin in these words: "God simply made me the instrument of his punishment. . . . I have too great a soul to die like a criminal. Oh may He, may He spare me that and let me die bravely!"

What a contrast to this passionate handwriting are the flowing, even words of Lincoln in another case! There on "Executive Mansion" stationery, in a modest, clear hand, are the memorable: ". . . that we here highly resolve that these dead shall not have died in vain; that this nation shall have a new birth of freedom; and that this government of the people, by the people, for the people, shall not perish from the earth."

The scene of Lincoln's death becomes real from a model of the theater in the museum. The stage was so deep that the boxes to left and right stared out on it like windows. The Presidential box on the upper right was draped with American flags. A blue Treasury Guards flag hung on the center pillar of the box, and an engraving of George Washington below it. The box was entered from the first balcony, through a small passage and a door. The narrow door, quite tall and bearing faded gray paint, is on exhibit at the museum.

Friday, April 14, 1865, as the newspapers on display show, was a day of peace and thanksgiving. Five days before, General Lee had surrendered at Appomattox. The war that had cleaved a nation and washed the battlefields with blood was coming to an end. Lincoln, to whom the war was an agony, was strangely exalted in these last days, as revealed in a photograph in the museum, taken four days before the assassination. His face was gaunt and he was thirty pounds underweight. But in the deepset eyes was the peace of one who sees the dawn, after a long night of suffering.

He was a lonely man whose mind traveled in strange places. Woodrow Wilson wrote of him:

"There is a very holy and very terrible isolation for the conscience of every man who seeks to read the destiny in the affairs of others. That privacy no man can intrude upon. That lonely search of the spirit for the right perhaps no man can assist. This strange child of the cabin kept company with invisible things, was born into no intimacy but that of its own silently assembling and deploying thoughts."

Alway there rode with Lincoln a mysterious foreboding, a series of dreams. One of his closest aides wrote: "He always believed that he would fall by the hand of an assassin, and yet with that appalling doom clouding his life — a doom fixed and irreversible, as he was firmly convinced — his courage never for a moment forsook him. . . . With that calm conviction which no philosophy could shake, Mr. Lincoln moved on through a maze of mighty events, calmly waiting the inevitable hour."

One night during the second week of April, Lincoln told his wife and a few friends of a vivid dream: "About ten days ago I retired very late. I had been up waiting for important dispatches from the front. I could not have been long in bed when I fell into a slumber, for I was very weary. I soon began to dream. There seemed to be a deathlike stillness about me. Then I heard subdued sobs, as if a number of people were weeping. I thought I left my bed and wandered downstairs. There the silence was broken by the same pitiful sobbing.

"I went from room to room; no living person was in sight, but the same mournful sounds of distress met me as I passed along. I was puzzled and alarmed. What could be the meaning of all this? I kept on until I arrived at the East Room, which I entered. There I met with a sickening surprise. Before me was a catafalque, on which rested a corpse wrapped in funeral vestments. Around it were stationed soldiers who were acting as guards, and there was a throng of people, some gazing mournfully on the corpse whose face was covered, others weeping pitifully.

"'Who is dead in the White House?' I demanded of one of the soldiers.

"'The President,' was his answer. 'He was killed by an assassin!'

"Then came a loud burst of grief from the crowd which awoke me from my dream. I slept no more that night; and although it was only a dream, I have been strangely annoyed by it ever since. . . ."

The President brooded a moment and said earnestly: "Well, let it go. I think the Lord in His own good time and way will work this out all right. God knows what is best."

On the afternoon of April 14, President Lincoln walked to the War Department with Colonel Crook, his aide and guard, and said soberly: "Do you know, I believe there are men who want to take my life? And I have no doubt they will do it. I have perfect confidence in every one of your men. But if it is to be done, it is impossible to prevent it."

That night was filled with one of the mists that unaccountably roll up from the Potomac and turn Washington into an eerie city of lights. Above, clouds drifted across the moon.

Fate intervened with a planned cunning. The assassin, being a well-known actor of the day, had easy access to the theater. Some time during the day, perhaps while Lincoln spoke with such feeling about his approaching death, Booth bored a hole in the inner door connecting the Presidential box with the passageway. Thus he could stand motionless in the dark, observing his prey until time to strike.

Booth never could have entered the box at 10:15 that night but for the curious selection of the Presidential guard, John Parker. He had been continually in trouble with the police board for drunkenness and neglect of duty. That night, he left his post for a drink. Then it was that Booth slipped into the passage, barred its outer door with a prop, and stood alone in the narrow space. He had reinforced his madness with a glass of whiskey at a saloon next door.

Lincoln, who had arrived late, sat back in a comfortable, red damask rocker with arm rests. Mrs. Lincoln was just ahead of him; Miss Clara Harris, a Senator's daughter, to the right of the President, and her fiancé, Major Henry Rathbone, assigned as a War Department guard, behind her.

Booth waited until a moment in the play when only one actor was on the stage. The actor was saying with an air of great good humor: "Well, I guess I know enough to turn you inside out, old gal, you sockdologizing old mantrap."

Booth crept into the box. In his right hand was a tiny pistol with a carved handle, a single-shot derringer. Today this instrument of tragedy seems so like a toy, smaller than a cap pistol, as it rests peaceably in a museum case. In Booth's left hand was a murderous dagger with a bone handle. The dagger, on display, looks cruel, cold and sharp.

Booth was both a coward and overstimulated. He aimed the derringer from behind at close range. But he miscalculated and, instead of hitting the planned area where death would be instant, the bullet entered above and to the right of Lincoln's left eye. The small bullet, a half-inch around, went diagonally and was lodged behind his right eye.

Lincoln sagged forward wordlessly in his chair. Major Rathbone, hardly knowing what had happened, lunged for the madman. With a savage strength no rational man could muster, Booth broke from the major and slashed him again and again with his knife. The dagger cut deep into the left arm above the elbow. Rathbone cried out desperately, "Stop that man!"

The museum visitor today can follow the story from the exhibits in the cases. There, behind glass, is the small, gracefully formed spur from Booth's left foot. Near it is the large Treasury Guards flag with the right lower corner torn out. There, too, are Booth's black boot, ripped down the center to free his injured leg; Booth's compass with the wax drippings from the candle he used to read it as he crossed the Potomac in the dark; his raving diary of the assassination and escape.

Booth, after freeing himself from Rathbone, jumped from the edge of the box to the stage. His right foot struck the Washington engraving, turning it over and slowing him enough for his spur to catch in the Treasury flag. The spur ripped the corner, and Booth fell awkwardly to the stage. He tore a hole in the green carpet. His left leg was fractured above the ankle.

Even so, the savage power of a lunatic bade him rise and cry hoarsely, "*Sic semper tyrannis!*" and, "The South is revenged!"

On his way out, Booth slashed at a man who stood in his way and clubbed a boy with the butt end of his knife.

Fate had no more use for Booth, now the deed was done, and he died a death as mean as his murder. Trapped in a Virginia barn, conscious and bleeding slowly to death, he passed unmourned. His accomplices in the plot to seize control of Washington (the Secretary of State was wounded in his sick room by a would-be assassin) were hanged.

In the theater, Mrs. Lincoln's screams, more than the shot, brought the hysteria of terror to the crowd. Some were paralyzed with fright, others stampeded to the exits to push and claw their way out. A few were curious and stood below the box. Troops were needed to restore order and empty the theater.

A young Army surgeon, Dr. Leale, was the first physician to arrive. As Fate would have it, Lincoln was his idol, and Dr. Leale did all man could do to relieve the suffering. While Mrs. Lincoln moaned, "Oh, Doctor, is he dead? Can he recover? Do what you can for him. Oh, my dear husband, my dear husband! — " Dr. Leale artificially restored regular breathing. He breathed directly into Lincoln's mouth and nostrils, and the panting movement of his lungs became regular. He removed a dangerous blood clot.

The leading lady of the stage had arrived in the box, and she held the bleeding head tenderly in her lap. Dr. Leale told Mrs. Lincoln, "The wound is mortal. He cannot recover."

Dr. Leale and two other physicians who had arrived decided that the dying man must be moved to the nearest bed. A fatal hemorrhage would be brought on by the bumpy carriage ride over cobblestones to the White House. So the unconscious Lincoln, like a giant fallen oak, was carried out of the darkened theater. Soldiers cleared the way; at first it was a crisp command, then as some stood stunned in the path, an angry, cursing cry to move. Four soldiers held the legs and trunk of the President, and a physician each his shoulders and his head.

The streets were filled with those brought running by the rumor spreading throughout downtown Washington. They saw the pitiful group. Here was the hero, the godly martyr, now a helpless fallen creature whose blood stained the hands of those who bore him.

There across the street was a simple, four-story home. It was a rooming house with a tailor shop in the lower floor, below street level. It was owned by William Petersen, a Swedish immigrant, a

Photo by Abbie Rowe — Courtesy National Park Service

frugal, hard-working tailor, the kind whom Lincoln was referring to when he wrote: "Labor is prior to, and independent of, capital. Capital is only the fruit of labor, and never could have existed if labor had not first existed. Labor is the superior of capital, and deserves much the higher consideration."

The seven men with their burden saw an open door and a figure with a light beckoning them. They mounted the nine curving steps, staggering with the effort to keep Lincoln's head up.

The visitor today can follow their path in the Petersen house. The furnishings within are similar to those that met the melancholy procession on Black Friday.

Lincoln was borne down the dark and narrow hall, past a hat rack and into the first bedroom. It is a small (ten paces long and five wide) room with a looped yarn rug on the worn wooden floor. The bed, with a cornhusk mattress, was just inside the door to the right. A print of "The Horse Fair" was on the wall over the bed, and one of "The Village Blacksmith" at the far end over a marble-topped wooden dresser. A bowl and pitcher rested on the wash-stand to the right below the bed. The two windows were curtained with a white material.

This room was rented to a soldier, a young private of Company D, 13th Massachusetts Infantry. Here again, perhaps, is the intervening hand of Fate. For Lincoln liked or disliked generals, according to the victories they won; but he had a compassion beyond any normal kindness for the enlisted man. He pardoned many sentenced to die or in prison for falling asleep on post after a hard day's march or battle.

The bed was too short for Lincoln's length. He was laid diagonally, completely unconscious but breathing regularly with an occasional deep sigh.

Mrs. Lincoln was assisted to the front parlor, another modest room with a black horsehair sofa, a few chairs, a small ornamental table and a fireplace. She was allowed to see her husband only after clean napkins were placed over the blood-stained pillow. She cried out in desperate pleading, "Live, you must live!" Hearing his loud, labored breathing, she fainted, and was carried to the sofa of the front parlor.

Just beyond, in the back parlor, the Cabinet met on call of the Secretary of War, Edwin M. Stanton. Here, Stanton issued orders to calm the excited nation. At the center table a corporal took evidence from witnesses to the crime.

The scene in the bedroom was almost like one copied from the Bible. A flickering gas light left dark shadows. The face of Lincoln was beautifully calm. His son Robert stood at the foot of the bed, at times unable to control his grief. Senator Charles Sumner sat with his sobbing head on the bed. Dr. Leale, who loved Lincoln, held the President's left hand, "to let him in his blindness know, if possible, he was in touch with humanity and had a friend."

Outside, a giant, uneasy crowd grew. The Negroes cried openly and unashamed. All during the dreadful night clouds rolled over the moon that some later recalled was red as blood.

At 1:30, when all hope was abandoned, Secretary Stanton wrote the formal notification of death of the President. From then on, the house was still but for muffled sobs.

Daylight came with a misty rain and a dampness that penetrated the house. A few gray shafts of daylight peered in dimly from the windows.

A doctor held a hand tenderly on the dying man's heart, waiting for the moment when it would cease to beat. One of those present at these last moments has remarked prayerfully of "a look of unspeakable peace" that settled on Lincoln's face.

At five seconds to 7:22, the heart was still, and the doctor lifted his face in the awful signal. The Reverend Phineas D. Gurley, pastor of the New York Avenue Presbyterian Church, whispered, "Let us pray!"

After the moment of silent worship, the gruff bearded Stanton, his face wet with tears, said softly: "Now he belongs to the ages!"

Hall of the Library of Congress

15. Culture of a Nation

THREE bronze doors on Capitol Hill guard an immense treasure — a treasure of more value to man than all the gold bars stored underground in Kentucky, or all the secrets locked in the vaults of the masters of war.

For, if God's wrath or man's ingenuity should destroy all the cities on earth, this treasure could rebuild a better world. This is the accumulated knowledge of mankind.

Behind the massive bronze doors of the Library of Congress is Learning . . . the awed wonder of a scholar in the Reading Room hunched over an ancient Bible, each letter written with loving care; the silent rapture of blind people reading Braille; maps traced on cowhide and used by the fearless explorers of long ago; great discoveries of the mind written in an exotic tongue on palm leaves.

One pilgrim from this storehouse of knowledge told fellow Senators what the library means to America: "Nothing can surpass it in importance. Knowledge is power, the power to maintain free government and preserve constitutional liberty. Without it, the world grows dark and the human race takes up its backward march to the regions of barbarism."

This shrine of learning is a granite building, whose dome is topped by the blazing torch of Learning. Behind the main library is a white stone annex where many of the world's great scholars spend their hours. The two buildings contain some 31,700,000 pieces . . . volumes, manuscripts, maps, pamphlets, reels of film, phonograph records, photographs and prints. In this vast collection and in the art throughout the Library, there is a source of fascination for all, even the child.

Children watch in delight the fountain outside the Library at street level. A bearded, lusty Neptune, King of the Sea, sits on a high bank of rocks while on either side a Triton blows a conch shell to summon water gods to the throne. Sea nymphs ride raging sea horses, and huge turtles and sea serpents loll in the sun.

Up above, along the window ledges, are the carved heads of all types of mankind, such as the blond European, Malay, Russian Slav, Semite, Zulu, Soudan Negro.

The sculptured bronze doors to the library relate the story of knowledge. One is Tradition — a mother telling her eager child of his father's deeds. Behind her, the pictured mountains gave one observer "a sense of prehistoric vastness and solitude."

Next is Printing — the Goddess of Learning, Minerva, and her winged messengers carrying folios. The third is Writing — a mother showing her children how to use the pen and scroll.

The visitor who passes through the deep arch into the marble entrance hall enters a forgotten dream. It is the dream of the young student who falls asleep over a book describing the age of learning five hundred years ago. All about are richly paneled walls, gilded ceilings, and statues. Here are the carved figures of Minerva in peace and war, a boy attentive over a book, an elderly bearded man deep in meditation, and up on the grand stairway, sculptured boys representing the continents.

Great treasures, belonging to all of us, are in cases around the balcony at the top of the stairs, free for any casual visitor to see. One is the first book printed in the Western World, the Gutenberg Bible. More than five hundred years ago, in the troubled medieval city of Mainz, Germany, Johann Gutenberg discovered movable type and printed more than two hundred Bibles in Latin. Some were on vellum, a fine soft animal skin that turns without a crackle; a few perfect copies survive. This is one of them.

Look well at it, the great glowing page alive with carved type, erect and clear, and rich in color. This book changed the life of man more than gunpowder or the atomic bomb, for it brought knowledge easily to all.

A few feet away is an example of an ancient art that died with Gutenberg's era. It is a huge Bible that a master scribe with a crow quill, and many illuminators with tiny brushes, working by sunlight and candle, spent fifteen months creating. Curiously, its time and birthplace were the same as the Gutenberg Bible. This was the gift of a wealthy merchant to his church, and each letter is a work of art; a sentence is a company of costumed soldiers marching elegantly across the stage. Some of the initials are of burnished gold leaf. The colors are soft, almost transparent.

The details of the drawings are so startlingly exact that the rose, for example, seems to unfold its beauty before the reader's eye; a nude woman nursing her baby is like a sharp vision from a dream. This is known as the Giant Bible of Mainz.

The visitor, moving slowly among the wood and glass cases, finds great moments in American history. Here is the strong hand of George Washington in a letter to his brother. He had just accepted command of the Army of Revolution, and wrote: "I am embarked on a wide ocean . . . from whence perhaps no safe harbour is to be found."

In another case in the writing of Thomas Jefferson is his passionate: "For I have sworn upon the altar of God eternal hostility against every form of tyranny over the mind of man."

A careful script in black ink on a sheet of White House notepaper says: "The day has come when America is privileged to spend her blood and her might for the principles that gave her birth and happiness and the peace she has treasured. God helping her, she can do no other." This is Woodrow Wilson's 1917 message to Congress.

In one of the last cases, handwritten words move with such feeling that they rise above the ruled lines. Here and there a word is crossed out and another written above it. This is Lincoln's writing . . . "that this nation, under God, shall have a new birth of freedom — and that this government of the people, by the people, for the people, shall not perish from the earth."

Photograph by the Library of Congress

Reading Room of the Library of Congress

Beyond this hall of treasures is the library's great heart, the Reading Room. The visitor who stands hushed in the gallery is like the traveler who sees a new land spread out below him from the mountain. Great writers from many lands have exclaimed over this huge circular room with its series of balconies, its dusky marble tiers, its statues, its amazing clock over the entrance. Displayed around the clock are the signs of the zodiac in bronze. Father Time, scythe in hand, stands erectly over the dial.

The Reading Room is filled with the soothing hum of fans, a smell of old books, and a rare emotion. It is as enveloping as love, as warm as courage, and as sacred as worship. This is the wonder and awe and elation of a reader discovering knowledge.

The visitor lingering on the balcony is moved by another observation — the search for knowledge is democratic. There below at desks worn and polished by use, are two nuns in black habit, a Negro boy lost in a volume opened before him, an elegantly dressed old lady turning pages, a Chinese in shirt sleeves, a typical college girl. This is their empire. None can disturb them here.

James Truslow Adams, in his *Epic of America,* gave the spirit of the chamber: "As one looks down on the general reading room, which alone contains 10,000 volumes which may be read without even asking, one sees the seats filled with silent readers, young and old, rich and poor, black and white, the executive and the laborer, the general and the private, the noted scholar and the school boy, all reading at their own library provided by their own democracy. It has always seemed to me a perfect working out in a concrete example of the American dream — the means provided by the accumulated resources of the people themselves, a public intelligent enough to use them, and men of high distinction, themselves a part of the great democracy, devoting themselves to the good of the whole."

Beyond the Reading Room, on the second floor, is a shrine, the Rare Books Division. Here, books as ancient as recorded history are treated with tenderness. The stilled room, where even a footstep intrudes, is modeled after Independence Hall, birthplace of American freedom. The bronze doors are emblazoned with the identifying marks of famous printers.

In the stacks of this Division are books that lit the flame of curiosity and sent explorers out into the world . . . the first edition of Homer in Greek; a small red and gold volume known to Columbus, the *Journey of Marco Polo;* the first British atlas on vellum; editions of a British printer who created a single English language; a letter of Columbus to the paymaster of the Spanish Court, describing his voyage to the "Islands of India."

Here, protected by a handsome leather case, is a rare curiosity dating to medieval times. It is a painstakingly copied script on vellum of *Journey to the Holy Land.* The author is the ancestor of today's science-fiction writer. He described in his bold imagination the monsters seen on this adventurous trip. On one page is a woodcut of a dog-faced monster, looking very like the creatures seen by today's writers on their imaginative rocket voyages to Venus.

Life moves forward in the stacks to the dawn of the United States and through its history. There is a collection of the books and writings of those who made America great. Here, at eye level, is a book of Abraham Lincoln's and in it a letter he wrote three years before he became President. "Our political problem now is can we live together half slave, half free. The problem is too weighty for me. May God in His Mercy superintend the solution."

The foundation of the Rare Books Division is the Thomas Jefferson Library. The student can find in this collection how Jefferson turned again and again to religious freedom. Lack of it had kept the world at war for centuries. In the books he read, in the comments he made, Jefferson sought a way to prevent religious strife. He found it in the Virginia Act establishing religious freedom.

Within the Jefferson correspondence in the Manuscript Division is a letter he wrote to James Madison, commenting on the publication in Europe of the Virginia Act. His serene, even script says:

"It is comfortable to see the standard of reason at length erected, after so many ages during which the human mind has been held in vassalage by kings, priests and nobles; and it is honorable for us to have produced the first legislature who has had the courage to declare that the reason of man may be entrusted with the formation of his own opinions."

Elsewhere in the Library, his undying words on learning and liberty call to the reader from the walls: "Educate and inform the mass of the people. Enable them to see that it is their interest to preserve peace and order, and they will preserve them. Enlighten the people generally, and tyranny and oppression of the body and mind will vanish like evil spirits at the dawn of today."

Jefferson's library, which he selected carefully in America and Europe and cataloged himself, is the basis for the Library of Congress. Actually, the library was founded as a footnote on an appropriation for furniture . . . "that for the purchase of such books as may be necessary for the use of Congress at the said city of Washington."

The capital then was still known to many by its Indian name of Conococheague. The books were stacked on the floor of an unused room in the Capitol and borrowed by those Congressmen who agreed with John Randolph that "a good library is a statesman's workshop."

In 1814, in retaliation for the American raid on Toronto (then York) and the burning of Parliament, the British burned the Capitol and with it the meager library. Jefferson thereupon offered to turn over his library to Congress at a reasonable cost. He wrote that it was "a collection . . . as probably never can again be effected, because it is hardly probable that the same opportunities, the same time, industry, perseverance and expense, with the same knowledge of the bibliography . . . would ever again be in concurrence."

A newspaper of the day proudly wrote: "It will remain for future generations an evidence of the literary treasures possessed by a man who had the honor of preparing the Declaration of Independence, and of the union of love of liberty and knowledge in our country. It is an honour to our country to say, that when a national collection was destroyed, the private Library of a President could supply its place."

Since those days, the Library of Congress has grown to the world's largest and most valuable collection, through copyright deposits, gifts and purchases. It has the largest number of books on Russia outside the Soviet Union, the greatest Oriental collection beyond China and Japan, nearly two million pieces of music, books in Braille and records for the blind that travel across the land to lighten lonely lives, miles of microfilm that can be viewed through special projectors, books that are weapons of war and instruments of peace.

In small air-conditioned niches in the Annex, scholars from almost every corner of the world pore over volumes, looking for some secret of life. The Copyright office is a huge assembly of Americana, from folk songs to the formula for an atomic fizz drink. Chamber music concerts are heard regularly in the auditorium, and conferences bring scholars for such topics as "Colloquium on Islamic Culture in Its Relation to the Contemporary World."

Yet even with this rare success, there remains a grave dilemma for the Library of Congress. How can this mass of wisdom, much of it created in the fires of pain and agony, be used by the world today? Must man in each generation learn the hard lessons of the past by cruel experience?

A few years ago, the then Librarian of Congress posed this riddle: "Our age is characterized by the tyranny of time. Time is running out, not like sand in a glass, but like the blood in an opened artery. There is still time left, but we can foresee clearly a moment when there will be none. . . . We will either educate the people of this Republic to know and value and preserve their own democratic culture, or we will watch the people of this Republic trade their democratic culture for the superstition, the brutality, the tyranny which is overrunning . . . Europe."

The Supreme Court

16. "No Justice Is God"

ONLY a grassy stretch, a few brooding old trees, and a street rattling with trolley cars separates a temple of white marble from the Capitol in Washington. Its steps sweep up grandly as though to a throne and touch majestic pillars which transform men into dwarfs. Across its brow are cut deep into stone the words: EQUAL JUSTICE UNDER LAW.

This is the Supreme Court, an institution as uniquely American as the "Battle Hymn of the Republic." It is the third great power of our government. It protects free men from prejudices that flame and die; it dares to defy tyrants who demand all power in their hands.

A visitor with some imagination might think of the Supreme Court as a modern Olympus. The courtroom is like an awe-filling church with an immense high ceiling. The chamber has twenty-four columns of tinted Italian marble, deep red drapes hanging the length of front and rear walls, ponderous copper gates and lattice on the sides, carved mahogany pews, and the long bench elevated so that a lawyer pleading a case looks up slightly to the eyes of the justices. Above the justices, etched in panels of marble, the gods of law — Hammurabi, Moses, Solomon, Confucius, Mohammed, Blackstone — stare down in judgment.

At the stroke of noon from the large copper-framed clock before the bench, nine black-robed justices enter in threes, through openings in the drapes. Clerks in frock coats and striped trousers bow low, and the Crier calls out, "Oyez, oyez, oyez! All persons having business before the Honorable, the Supreme Court of the United States, are

Photograph from the Library of Congress

admonished to draw near and give their attention, for the Court is now sitting. God save the United States and this honorable Court!"

The illusion that this is a mystic shrine where people pray in a strange tongue lingers while lawyers plead their cases with technical words and phrases. But it disappears swiftly when the justices ask questions. Law and justice are human, instead of being creatures of pomp and ritual. Some questions from the justices are blunt, to match the man in the robe; others kindly, sarcastic, bored, labored — as the temperaments of the Nine behind the bench vary.

The full tale of the Court's human qualities is hidden in the hushed and splendid law library two floors above, and in the portraits of justices adorning the walls of conference rooms. There, over the inner door of the lawyers' lounge, is a small portrait with a dramatic story.

Look closely at the old-fashioned painting — the clear eyes of a man who will not surrender, a determined yet not hostile jaw, a strong nose and wide forehead, the casual dress of one indifferent to personal show, and the same look of lonely leadership as that borne by Abraham Lincoln.

This is a profile of John Marshall, who was not afraid to find new paths and who stood by his beliefs against the tumult of the mob. Demagogues ranted against Marshall, excited crowds hung him in effigy, and a President and Congress threatened him, but he stood like a rock. Today, thanks to him, the rights of men in the United States cannot be burned away by the fevers of politics or chained by would-be czars in public office.

The words that John Marshall spoke from the bench of the Supreme Court in the early, insecure days of the Republic are still alive: "The very essence of civil liberty certainly consists in the right of every individual to claim the protection of the laws whenever he receives an injury. One of the first duties of government is to afford that protection. . . . "

Marshall was a backwoods patriot, with only a few weeks' formal schooling in law. He fought with George Washington and suffered the miseries of that forlorn army. He saw the Revolutionary troops held together only by faith in freedom, while legislatures wrangled endlessly and profiteers fattened in the cities.

Later, Marshall saw the French Revolution turn into an orgy of revenge and tyranny by the mob. From these experiences was born a conviction "that without a strong and practical government, democracy cannot solve its giant problems and orderly liberty cannot live."

President Adams, as one of his last acts, appointed his Secretary of State, Marshall, to the Court where he became Chief Justice. The court then was as weak as a sapling in a windstorm. It was loaded with Federalists, some of whom denounced the Jeffersonians in political speeches from the bench. Others were timid. None thought to say whether a law was legal. The Supreme Court only *interpreted*.

Marshall created a new and enduring philosophy — that the Constitution was a "superior, paramount law." The Constitution was like a house: the rooms and doors and closets could be altered to fit the needs and styles of new occupants, but only if this did not weaken the frame. Then the house would fall.

Marshall acted boldly at a time when the Supreme Court was under heavy fire. Two justices had been impeached by Congress. His political enemies waited for the slightest slip to try Marshall. In the famous Marbury *vs.* Madison case, Marshall declared a law *unconstitutional* because it violated the Constitution. And to this day, this power over Congress remains inviolate.

Marshall's decision brought grumblings from opposition leaders, but it was too remote from daily life to rouse the people as did his trial of Aaron Burr. The suave Burr, a former Vice President, was persecuted as an act of political revenge. He was accused of treason: mob spirit demanded his head.

In court, Marshall condemned "public feelings which may be and often are artificially excited against the innocent, as well as the guilty . . . a practice not less dangerous than it is criminal."

When Burr was acquitted, Marshall was excoriated in the press and hung in effigy by rioters. But he created a deathless principle that protects the humblest citizen today.

In the room next to the Marshall portrait, a twinkling old gentleman, Justice Oliver Wendell Holmes, Jr., looks from the wall with the good humor of one who loves and understands life. He sits black-robed in his chair, white hair neatly parted, gallant mustache flourishing grandly. Holmes's personality speaks in that mustache. It is not the stiff Prussian kind with the arrogant upturned ends, nor the dandy's slim, waxed adornment. This is friendly, and worn with the air of one who secretly enjoys the startled awe it creates.

The gift to freedom of this New Englander is not that he led the Court in great new decisions, for Holmes was the great dissenter, sparkling with wit and logic and a sense of his time. Holmes's gift was fourfold. He gave life and breath to law at a time when the Supreme Court had become stuffy with pomp. He threw open the door for reforms of the Industrial Age. He re-created a fervor for freedom of speech. And he gave us an undying faith in the future.

"Law is human," Holmes said. "It is a part of man, and of one world with all the rest. The very considerations which judges most rarely mention . . . are the secret root from which the law draws all the juices of life. I mean consideration of what is expedient for the community."

In showing that our Constitution is broad enough to serve new times, Holmes wrote: "A Constitution is not intended to embody a particular economic theory. It is made for people of fundamentally differing views, and the accident of our finding certain opinions natural and familiar, or novel and even shocking, ought not to conclude our judgment upon the question whether statutes embodying them conflict with the Constitution."

After World War I, suspicion closed over men of differing ideas. One extremist, whose ideas were said by Holmes to "drool a creed of immaturity," attracted far greater attention than his foolish pamphlets when he was sentenced to twenty years' imprisonment for distributing them. When the case came before the Court, Justice Holmes in the minority said:

"Congress certainly cannot forbid all effort to change the mind of the country. When men have realized that time has upset many fighting faiths, they may come to believe that the best test of truth is the power of the thought to get itself accepted in the competition of the market."

Deep within him, Holmes had a glorious faith in mankind — a faith that can give hope today to men frightened by the horrors of war. He said thoughtfully: "I do not pin my dreams for the future to my country or even to my race. I think it probable that civilization will last as long as I care to look ahead — perhaps with smaller numbers, but perhaps also bred to greatness and splendor by science.

"I think it not improbable that man, like the grub that prepares a chamber for the winged thing it never has seen but is to be — that man may have cosmic destinies that he does not understand. And so beyond the vision of battling races and an impoverished earth, I catch a dreaming glimpse of peace."

When he was Chief Justice, the dignified Charles Evans Hughes would sit alone in the conference room until afternoon faded into dusk and the lights came on outside. At such times, he mused over the problems of law, and remembered what he had written:

"The Supreme Court is the assurance that in the complexities of an extraordinary expanded life, we have not forgotten the ancient faith by which we have pledged ourselves to render each one his due."

Today's visitor to the big white building will sense that each justice is a mortal, with the likes and dislikes that man is prey to, yet guided by an awesome sense of duty. Indeed, they should remember that one justice, answering the question, "What advice would you give future members of the Supreme Court?" smiled and replied:

"I would remind him of what Mr. Holmes once said: 'No Justice is God. He is a man serving men.' "

Photograph from the Library of Congress

Lafayette Park

17. Glory and Grandeur

ON the glorious days which Indian summer brings to Washington, an older man rests on a park bench across from the White House. He looks thoughtfully at the pillared entrance to the Executive Mansion, or watches with amusement as squirrels at his feet scamper for peanuts.

Every new breath of wind showers leaves about him from the graceful arms of an ancient elm. A few feet away, a young sailor sprawls gratefully in the warm sun, two lovers walk hand in hand by a garden of brilliant flowers, and happy children skip down the curving walk while their mothers look on proudly. A pigeon waddles up, cooing for crumbs.

The park-bench philosopher may be an elder statesman, like Bernard Baruch, thinking out a plan for peace; a Cabinet member escaping from his office; or a kindly retired government clerk with a paper sack of bread scraps.

This haven for philosophers, lovers and children is Lafayette Park, often called "The Lobby of the White House." It is filled and surrounded by omens of a glory that never dies . . . a spirited Andrew Jackson greeting his troops at the Battle of New Orleans and reining a fiercely rearing horse . . . the gas-lit house where a bold naval hero fell dying after a duel . . . the faded grandeur of a gracious mansion where a beautiful woman once ruled Washington . . . a serene church where Presidents have bowed their heads in silent prayer.

This seven acres of monuments, rare trees and flowers, a rectangle parallel to the White House across Pennsylvania Avenue, is an

American common, like a village courthouse square. In moments of great national joy or sorrow, Lafayette Park suddenly fills like a stream at flood tide.

Wildly celebrating crowds trampled the flowers and cheered their hero when Jackson, first avowed champion of the common man, was inaugurated. More than a century later, on a warm April afternoon, silent thousands stood numb with sorrow in Lafayette Park. A few moved their lips in prayer, "The Lord is my shepherd . . . " Another favorite of the masses, Franklin D. Roosevelt, had passed away in a Georgia cottage, after writing these words:

"The only limit to our realization of tomorrow will be our doubts of today. Let us move forward with a strong and active faith."

Somehow, Lafayette Park is a well where the weary and disillusioned can drink deeply of faith. Forty different types of trees, some as exotic as a Persian garden, shade the wanderer. Elms older than memory guard the border. There is a startling and tall bald cypress whose green-needled limbs shape to a cone at the top . . . a Chinese scholar tree with pods like amber beads . . . giant, shiny leafed magnolias with fragrant white flowers . . . spreading purple beeches. Flowers, gardens, changing with the seasons, are as full of color as the rainbow.

Four ardent lovers of liberty greet the day at the corners of Lafayette Park. These tall statues are of men who came to the New World from Europe, to fight for an ideal that Jefferson captured with words in the Declaration of Independence. At the southeast corner stands an elegant Lafayette, the devoted young French nobleman who served on Washington's staff; at the other corner on Pennsylvania Avenue, the Count de Rochambeau, wily old French general who led four thousand of France's best troops in the Revolutionary War and devised strategy for Washington; at the northwest corner, General Von Steuben, the Prussian officer who in 1776 trained raw recruits into fighting men; and, at the northeast, General Thaddeus Kosciuszko, the Pole, is shown as he holds plans for the fortifications he drew at Saratoga. These figures are reminders of our eternal debt to men everywhere who yearn for freedom.

The walks of Lafayette Park radiate from the remarkable equestrian statue of Jackson in the center. This is a stern, strong-willed, battle-tense Jackson. The statue is cast of bronze Spanish cannons that Jackson captured in battle. Four of these same cannon, green with the kindly passage of time, surround the statue.

On the pedestal, the curious visitor can read Old Hickory's motto: OUR FEDERAL UNION, IT MUST BE PRESERVED.

Long before Jackson was fighting at New Orleans, the site of Lafayette Park was a farm whose acres were occasionally wet by overflows of the broad Potomac River. When George Washington chose this site at the same time he picked the ground for the President's house, the tract included a farmhouse, an apple orchard, and a small family graveyard. One legend says Washington at that time named the park for his protégé Lafayette.

While the White House was being built, the temporary workmen's quarters were here. Jefferson, with his extraordinary talent for landscaping, ordered the area laid out into a formal park. A few years later, British troops tramped across these peaceful grounds on their way to burn the White House.

Only eleven years distant, in Monroe's "era of good feeling," Lafayette Square (the park with the buildings surrounding it) was the center of the plots and counterplots that always form the tumult of Washington. In the celebrated boarding house to the east of the Park, in the elegant Arlington Hotel to the north, in the mansions — Blair House, Decatur House, Dolly Madison House, Corcoran House, and Ashburton House — the political and social life swirled in a giddy pace.

A celebrated epicurean, polished Baron Von Tuyl, the Russian Minister, said in delight: "Washington with its venison, wild turkey, canvasback ducks, oysters and terrapins furnishes better viands than Paris." A later observer wrote in awe of a banquet given by Andrew Carnegie at the Arlington Hotel: "It far excelled the feast of Lucullus in his villa at Tuscalum."

On the southeast corner of Lafayette Square, where the Treasury

Annex sits today like a prim and proper bank teller, was the home of a dentist who ministered to Presidential toothaches, Thomas S. Gunnell. One morning, an excited White House messenger, his coat tails flying, bade Dr. Gunnell to hurry to President Martin Van Buren. The dentist seized his drills and tools, but found the President waiting with a reward for his expert attention — the job as Postmaster of the District of Columbia.

A door north, where the old Belasco Theater stands (now a USO theater), was a boarding house. It was an arena for the great debates that drew the nation into civil war. The ground was originally swapped from Henry Clay for an Andalusian jackass, a deal with which the Washington wits had great fun. One of those who stomped in to breakfast of ham and griddle cakes was John C. Calhoun, erect, fiery-eyed, with a fiercely upright shock of hair and a voice that rang with passion. He was the South's champion in the Senate.

Another guest was the great compromiser, Senator Henry Clay, whose temperate appeals held off war for a few years. A third boarder was long-faced Chief Justice Roger B. Taney of the Supreme Court. It was Taney's Dred Scott decision, labeling slaves as "articles of merchandise" rather than people, that so aroused the North.

History lived with this house, for later it became the home of Lincoln's Secretary of State, William H. Seward. Five days after General Lee surrendered at Appomattox, on Black Friday, a conspirator broke into the house and slashed the Secretary with a bowie knife. Seward lived, but Lincoln, shot by a crazed actor a few blocks away, died.

A smaller building crouching to the north was known in its hours of glory as "The Little White House." It was the residence of Mark Hanna, tough-minded Republican boss who came out of the pages of a novel. He was a Cleveland millionaire who made his fortune from coal, iron and newspapers, was frank to the point of bluntness, and had a firm jaw and clear, shrewd eyes. Hanna believed absolutely in the idea, "What is good for business is good for America."

He organized business to defeat the "radical" William Jennings

Bryan and elect "safe" William McKinley. Hanna then sat in his mansion, a few steps from the White House, and guided the affairs of state. Administration policies were rounded out at breakfasts of cornbeef hash in "The Little White House," attended by Cabinet officers and Congressional leaders.

On the northeast corner of Lafayette Square, the beautiful Dolly Madison won men's minds by a dimpled smile, a creamy skin and haunting blue eyes. The "Madison House," now a grimy gray with traces of the old finery in the delicate iron lattice work on the side facing the Square, was Madison's residence when he was Jefferson's Secretary of State.

Dolly was eighteen years younger than her husband, wore rouge and daring low-cut gowns. In rooms where government typists sit sedately today, Dolly danced with the enraptured Senators and secretaries, and won favors for her husband.

Until recent years, the Madison and Hanna residences were the time-mellowed chambers of the dignified Cosmos Club, of which Washington wags are wont to say: "The Cosmos Club has brains, but no money; the Metropolitan Club money, but no brains; the University Club, neither." Today, government clerks fill the rooms, never suspecting the history which the walls have seen.

On the Square's north rim, the gray Veterans Administration building squats on ground where the elegant Arlington Hotel opened its doors. Many Presidents-elect quartered there awaiting Inauguration, and looked curiously across the square at the white mansion where their fame would be made or lost. Cabinet dinners were held in its private dining rooms, and lobbyists stalked its fern-decorated lobby, searching for prey.

To the west still stands a regal brownstone mansion. Compared to the more modern architecture of downtown Washington, this solid and formal structure looks like a character out of Dickens. Actually, it was here that Lord Ashburton, the British Minister, wined and dined with Secretary of State Daniel Webster. The two planned the future world to be organized under the benevolent guidance of an Anglo-American alliance. This alliance, the Webster-

Ashburton Treaty of 1842, was sealed at famous dinners of statesmen at this regal mansion of Lord Ashburton, and has stood for
more than a century.

Secretary Webster, who lived a few doors down the street in the
magnificent Corcoran House, waged a battle of chefs with Ashburton. Their tables groaned with such delicacies as South Carolina
rice birds, Parisian potages, champagne and Burgundy.

Today, as if to reveal the change of forces dominating Washington, the Ashburton House is the office of the American Federation
of Labor's League for Political Education. Machinists and carpenters
and printers, bent on making the ballot box their weapon, come and
go through doors once filled by the shadows of nobility.

A hotel now occupies the space taken up by an imposing stone
castle, the twin residence of John Hay, Lincoln's private secretary
and Secretary of State for two Presidents, and Henry Adams, writer
and historian. Here was written an authoritative biography of
Lincoln and *The Education of Henry Adams*.

The United States Chamber of Commerce busies itself in a gleaming white palace on the site of the Corcoran House. This latter was
celebrated as "the most splendid town establishment in the country,"
and was built by his patrons for Webster, who would have been
an admirable Cosmos Club member. After a short period in this
elegant establishment, Webster regretfully gave it up as too ex-
pensive.

The northwest corner of the Square is occupied even today by a
fabulous house — red brick with green shutters, built flush to the
sidewalk. This is the Decatur House, designed by the most famous
architect of the time, Latrobe, and paid for by the prize money that
Commodore Stephen Decatur won driving the Barbary pirates from
the seas.

Within, the Decatur House has tall windows, iron balconies, large
rooms separated by archways, lighted chandeliers hanging from
frescoed ceilings, a two-room library filled with rare volumes, and
beautifully carved mantels.

When Decatur had lived there less than a year, he left his anxious bride to fight a duel at the Blandensburg dueling field, not far distant in Maryland. He staggered back to Decatur House to die. The duel with Commodore James Barron was the aftermath of a controversial court-martial.

Later, so the legend goes, the north windows of Decatur House were bricked up on complaint of passers-by. They swore that after dark, the ghost of Decatur stood in an upstairs window and shouted salty oaths at them.

A later resident was Martin Van Buren, who, as Vice President, was supposed to have ordered windows cut in the south wall so that he might watch signals from the White House.

In later days, an invitation to dinner at Decatur House was as prized as a private audience with a king. Mrs. Truxton Beale, leader of a small, elite circle of Washington society, which scorned the passing parade of politicians, was hostess to the initiates. The house, even as in the Commodore's day, was never a glare of electric lights. Gas lights, lamps and candles threw a mellow glow over the lovely rooms.

The rear of Decatur House, once the slave quarters, is now a Naval Museum, watched over by a faithful enlisted man.

A trim row of buildings down the west side of the Square house such a variety of modern organizations as the National Grange, CIO, International Bank, and Brookings Institution. Around the corner is the Blair-Lee House, home of Presidential guests.

Yet time has not touched the peace and beauty of the oldest structure on the Square. Its simple spire rises calmly like a distant mountain above the busy clatter of footsteps and sweeping trees. Its ancient bell rings out sweet and true over the roar of traffic. This is St. John's, "The Church of Presidents." A grateful worshiper has described it as "a place where there is a subduing sense of eternal things."

Today, as in generations past, men and women of all rank sit and kneel in this quiet, small temple. They are there from early morning until after the long shadows of sunset on the park have faded into

night. They are in search of peace, and find it in the belief, "In God We Trust."

Lincoln came down from the sad heights of lonely power to fold his long legs into a rear pew. He would leave quietly before the evening service was ended and walk back across the park in the dusk. The soft voice of the unseen organ, the great poetry of the Bible, the sound of birds in the park, gave him new strength.

In other hours of crisis, Woodrow Wilson's taut face relaxed in St. John's; Franklin Roosevelt entered the church an hour before his first Inauguration to pray; Harry Truman, troubled by the dilemmas of the atomic bomb and Korea, walked across the park in the morning while the grass was still wet with dew.

Many Presidents, from Madison down, were regular members of the congregation and sat in the narrow, cloth-covered pew on the left aisle. It is found by a small disc with the numbers "54." Every President since its founding has discovered the peculiar power of the church across the Square. President McKinley, for one, would wheel his chair to a window in the White House study so he could see St. John's spire. Often he said that the sight soothed and comforted him.

The church has been a part of our national life since 1816. The White House was still standing half-burnt when architect Latrobe designed St. John's. The bell, whose even tones ring out across the Square every noon, was fashioned in the Revere foundry of cannons captured from the British.

Today, the visitor will find St. John's as it was in Madison's day. The open doors beyond the great pillars are a welcome to men of all faiths. Within, a few sit with bowed heads in the stately box pews whose wooden arms are worn by the touch of a century. The flames of tall white candles on either side of the altar bend in a breeze. The stained-glass window is of Christ and His Disciples. A great red Bible rests on a pedestal that is formed by the widespread metal wings of an eagle.

From one side, softly, gently, come the swelling tones of an organ in a familiar hymn. Few effects of man give such peace as the sound of an organ in an almost deserted church. Here in this temple, to those absorbed in meditation, is a nation's prayer:

> *Though like a wanderer*
> *The sun gone down*
> *Darkness comes over me,*
> *My rest a stone;*
> *Yet in my dreams I'd be*
> *Nearer, my God, to Thee,*
> *Nearer to Thee!*